# Praise for *Living an Examined Life*

"*Living an Examined Life* is a gift of rare gold: the accumulated logos of a life lived deeply and fully, generously shared and beautifully crafted. James Hollis bridges profound psychological insight and practical application. Joyously, this book dares us to go beyond the ordinary acknowledgement of the terrors of the adventure before us, yet promises—like a loyal, loving, trusty Sherpa—to accompany us as we navigate the difficult terrain of authentic personal growth. This is *the* book to have as a fellow traveler—Socratic interrogator, wise friend, loving teacher, mindful mentor."

**MARTIN LLOYD-ELLIOTT**
psychologist, psychotherapist, author

"This book represents the distillation of a lifetime's accumulated wisdom. The reader is sure to find helpful guidance for life's perplexities and warm companionship on the way."

**LIONEL CORBETT**
professor at Pacifica Graduate Institute

"Nobody writes about the challenges of creating a meaningful life with as much wisdom and warmth as James Hollis. This book is an extraordinary gift to all of us grappling with the 'second half of life'—free of all platitudes and false comforts, but full of sustenance, humor, and tools for navigating the journey."

**OLIVER BURKEMAN**
columnist for the *Guardian* and author of *The Antidote: Happiness for People Who Can't Stand Positive Thinking*

"This is a book full of gems. Some are wise, some are deep, some are precious. Still others are even funny and others self-evident. Yet every one of them is necessary and belongs to the whole. As if James Hollis had scanned the inner landscape of us all, himself included, to produce a necklace of human truths from every part of the psyche, including the wondrous, the normal, and the dire. Reading him is to be reminded that it is possible to be fully human because—and not in spite of—our full part of light and shadow."

JAN BAUER
Jungian analyst and author of
*Impossible Love: Or Why the Heart Must Go Wrong*

"James Hollis is the most lucid thinker I know about the complexities and complexes that interfere with living a full life. His broad background in literature, philosophy, and Jungian psychology is everywhere present in this important book, which, as it strips away illusions, posits the soul-work that's necessary for the difficult task of making our lives meaningful. He's one of our great teachers and healers."

STEPHEN DUNN
Pulitzer Prize–winning poet

# Living an
# EXAMINED
# LIFE

# Also by James Hollis

*Harold Pinter: The Poetics of Silence*

*The Middle Passage: From Misery to Meaning at Midlife*

*Under Saturn's Shadow: The Wounding and Healing of Men*

*Tracking the Gods: The Place of Myth in Modern Life*

*Swamplands of the Soul: New Life in Dismal Places*

*The Eden Project: In Search of the Magical Other*

*The Archetypal Imagination*

*Creating a Life: Finding Your Individual Path*

*On This Journey We Call Our Life: Living the Questions*

*Mythologems: Incarnations of the Invisible World*

*Finding Meaning in the Second Half of Life:
How to Finally, Really Grow Up*

*Why Good People Do Bad Things: Understanding Our Darker Selves*

*What Matters Most: Living a More Considered Life*

*Hauntings: Dispelling the Ghosts Who Run Our Lives*

# *Living an* EXAMINED LIFE

Wisdom for the
Second Half of the Journey

## James Hollis, PhD

**sounds true**
BOULDER, COLORADO

Sounds True, Inc.
Boulder, CO 80306

Published 2018

This work is solely for personal growth and education. It should not be treated as a
substitute for professional assistance, therapeutic activities such as psychotherapy
or counseling, or medical advice. In the event of physical or mental distress,
please consult with appropriate health professionals. The application of protocols
and information in this book is the choice of each reader, who assumes full
responsibility for his or her understandings, interpretations, and results. The author
and publisher assume no responsibility for the actions or choices of any reader.

Cover design by Karen Polaski
Book design by Beth Skelley

Cover images © mcherevan, © George_C, Shutterstock

Printed in the United States of America

Library of Congress Cataloging-in-Publication Data
Names: Hollis, James, 1940- author.
Title: Living an examined life: wisdom for the second half of the journey /
    James Hollis, PhD.
Description: Boulder, CO : Sounds True, Inc., [2018] | Includes
    bibliographical references.
Identifiers: LCCN 2017017881 (print) | LCCN 2017033164 (ebook) |
    ISBN 9781683640486 (ebook) | ISBN 9781683640479 (paperback)
Subjects: LCSH: Self-perception. | Self-realization. | Maturation (Psychology)
Classification: LCC BF724.85.S43 (ebook) | LCC BF724.85.S43 H653 2018 (print) |
    DDC 155.6/69—dc23
LC record available at https://lccn.loc.gov/2017017881

FSC
www.fsc.org
MIX
Paper | Supporting
responsible forestry
FSC® C103098

For Jill,
for Taryn, and Jonah, and Seah,
and Tim, always Tim with me.
And my thanks to
Liz Harrison, agent and friend,
and
Gretel Hakanson, editor and friend.

# Contents

Preface . . . ix

CHAPTER 1  The Choice Is Yours . . . 1

CHAPTER 2  It's Time to Grow Up . . . 7

CHAPTER 3  Let Go of the Old . . . 13

CHAPTER 4  Recover Personal Authority . . . 19

CHAPTER 5  Seek to Make Amends . . . 25

CHAPTER 6  Step Out from under the Parental Shade . . . 29

CHAPTER 7  Vow to Get Unstuck . . . 33

CHAPTER 8  Come Back to Your Task . . . 39

CHAPTER 9  Choose the Path of Enlargement . . . 45

CHAPTER 10  What Gift Have You Been
Withholding from the World? . . . 51

CHAPTER 11  See the Old Self-Destructive Patterns . . . 57

CHAPTER 12  What Is the Bigger Picture for You? . . . 63

CHAPTER 13  Choose Meaning over Happiness . . . 69

CHAPTER 14  Honor, Finally, What You Left Behind,
and Seize Permission to Be Who You Are . . . 75

CHAPTER 15  Exorcise the Ghosts of the Past That Bind You . . . 81

CHAPTER 16  Free Your Children from You . . . 87

CHAPTER 17  Bestow Love on the Unlovable Parts of You . . . 91

CHAPTER 18  Honor the Difference
between Job, Duty, and Calling . . . 97

CHAPTER 19  Construct a Mature Spirituality . . . 103

CHAPTER 20  Seize Permission to Be Who You Really Are . . . 109

CHAPTER 21  Live the Examined Life:
Live the Questions, Not the Answers . . . 115

Afterword . . . 119

Notes . . . 121

Bibliography . . . 123

About the Author . . . 125

# Preface

I offer this book containing the summation of decades of working with students, clients, analysands, and myself in the hope that it will be helpful to each reader in the conduct of his or her life and bring a greater sense of purpose and personal permission to be, in the end, who he or she is. All that sounds so simple, but in fact it is very difficult.

For the last thirty years, I have had the privilege of traveling to four continents giving presentations and workshops and have flown well over a million miles to these scattered venues. As a result, I have witnessed what touches people, what energizes them, what reminds them of something they know but perhaps have forgotten, and finally, what challenges them to come back to their journey. Herein I summarize these very complex issues in a finite list of graspable points. Sometimes we need a list, sometimes to be reminded, and sometimes to be kicked in the butt. This book is that reminder, that kick in the butt. This book promises nothing easy. It asks that the reader be serious about looking at his or her life and taking responsibility for it. We are, after all, the only constant character in that long-running soap opera we call our life. Therefore, it might well be argued that we are somehow accountable for how it is turning out.

This book contains twenty-one desiderata, the daily acknowledgment of which will change your life, make it more interesting, make it more nearly your own, and make possible the recovery of your journey.

It is my surmise that you have not picked up this book idly or as a distraction. You have done so out of a nagging curiosity, a deep, abiding pain, an unresolved life problem. Moreover, you most likely want surcease of suffering, rapid improvement, and abiding change for the better. If someone tells you the truth—that you will likely be dealing with these issues most of your life, that you will come back to them over and over in new venues, new relationships, new stages of life—you would likely move on quickly. But the truth is the truth, and as Jung pointed out, we seldom solve problems, but we can outgrow them. That is what this book is about, not solutions, but attitudes, behaviors, and disciplines that move us toward enlargement, toward enfolding our debilitating history into a journey more productive, more clearly our own. As I believe these ideas require reflection, percolation through the layers of our accumulated resistance to change, *I strongly recommend that the book not be read straight through, but a chapter a day. Only a disciplined reading allows the ideas to percolate to our soul.* To that end, the chapters have been kept short and to the point. Reading one chapter per day allows greater absorption than surfing through the whole permits.

It is my hope that this book will be a tool for each of us to recover respect for that which abides deeply within. As we do, we will not be spared disappointment or suffering, but we will know the depth and dignity of an authentic journey, of being a real player in our brief moment on this turning planet, and our life will become more interesting to us, taking us deeper than ever before. Only then are we on the journey of the soul. As the Danish theologian Kierkegaard observed: merchant mariners get their sailing orders in the safe harbor; men-o'-war open their instructions on the high seas. Whether you know it or not, you are on the high seas of the soul and have been so for a long time. It is time to open our instructions, set a new course, turn and tack into the wind, and sail onward, with the destination unfolding as we move.

**James Hollis,**
Washington, DC

# Chapter 1

# The Choice Is Yours

We are flung from the amniotic sea into this life—tied to matter, to gravity, to mortality. A fire burns in each of us, a tungsten intensity that flares and flames awhile and then departs. From whence and whither to remain mysteries. And who we are on this planet, and for what purpose, remains a mystery as well. Although the world is full of people who will tell you who you are, what you are, and what you are to do and not to do, they wander amid their unaddressed confusion, fear, and need for consensual belief to still their own anxious journey.

Whether you show up as you in this brief transit we call life or are defined by history, or context, or shrill partisan urgencies substantially depends on you. No greater difficulty may be found than living this journey as mindfully, as accountably, as we can, but no greater task brings more dignity and purpose to our lives. Swimming in this milky sea of mystery, we long to make sense of things, figure out who we are, wither bound, and to what end, while the eons roll on in their mindless ways. It falls then to us to make sense of this journey.

So what could be more obvious than point one: *the choice is ours.* And yet, is it? We survive in this life by adaptation. We learn from our world—families of origin, popular culture, world events, religious training, and many other sources—who we are, what is acceptable, what is not, and how we have to behave, perform, in order to fit in, gain approval from others, and prosper in this world into which we were thrust. Historically, all cultures have claimed that their values, their institutions, their marching orders come from the gods, sacrosanct scriptures, and venerated institutions. These "givens" are laden with presumptive powers and punitive sanctions for transgressions of any kind. A child raised today in the world of virtual reality and video games is just as susceptible to these acculturating and directive images. We become too often a servant of our environment, given our need to fit in, receive the approval of others, stay out of harm's way.

When I was a child in the 1940s, for example, there were pretty clear social definitions of gender, of social and economic class, of racial, ethnic, religious identity, and defined acceptable choices. To deviate from these prescriptive templates was to trigger sanctions of enormous proportion. The most common socializing sentence my contemporaries and I heard was, "What would people think?" A familiar proverb in Japan declares, "It is the protruding nail that gets hammered." In the face of such sanctioning power, what child does not begin to adopt the prejudices of his family and tribe, fear the alien values of others, and stick close to home in almost every way?

Since the 1940s and '50s, all of those categories, reportedly created by the gods themselves, have been deconstructed. While sex is biologically driven, gender is socially construed, and constricting definitions for men and women then have proved still another of many frangible fictions. Today we know that the range of choices for any of us is infinitely greater. We know that all races are mixed, that genetically we track back to a few progenitors in central Africa. We know that religions are mostly mythosocial constructs that arise out of tribal experiences that are institutionalized to preserve and to transmit and that the ontological claims of one tribe are no better, really, than the mythosocial constructs of other tribes. We know further that social practices, ethical prescriptions, are subjective value percepts and have no authority outside our tribe. Such a thought would have led any of us to the stake in an earlier era, and still will in many quarters.[1] When an idea occurs as an alternative, forces within the psyche rise to combat it, for our egos are very insecure and prefer clarity, authority, and control at all costs.

To say that any of us has a choice, really, is still a dubious statement. While we celebrate social license, revel in eccentricity, and accept changing social structures, reports from the behaviorists and the neurologists and the geneticists narrow the window of freedom more and more. In fact, the older I get, the narrower that window has become, despite having spent a life in education, in study, travel, and reflection. The powers of the unconscious cannot be underestimated. Our ego consciousness—namely, who we think we are, or what we believe real—is at best a thin wafer floating on an iridescent sea. In any moment, we view the world through a distorting lens and make choices based on what the lens allows us to see, not what lies outside its frame.

The more conscious we become, the more we become aware of unconscious influences working upon our daily choices. Why did you make that choice and not another at a critical juncture in your life? Why hook up with that person? Why repeat those family-of-origin patterns? These are disconcerting questions, but unless we ask them, we remain at the mercy of whatever forces are at work autonomously within us. These confrontations with the ego's fantasy of sovereignty are truly intimidating, but they remain a summons to greater awareness. How haunting is Carl Jung's observation that whatever is denied within us is likely to come to us in the outer world as fate? (That thought alone keeps me at this work.)

I am not in any way suggesting that our cultural values, our religious traditions, our communal practices are wrong; that is not for me to judge. Many of those values link us with community, give us a sense of belonging and guidance in the flood of choices that beset us daily. I am saying, however, that the historic powers of such expectations, admonitions, and prohibitions are to be rendered conscious, considered thoughtfully, and tested by the reality of our life experience and inner prompting. No longer does received authority—no matter how ratified by history, sanctioned by tradition—automatically govern. We are rather called to a discernment process. We are summoned to ask such questions as: Does this align with or make sense of my experience? If not, it may be well intended and right for someone else, but it is not right for me. Does this value, practice, or expectation take me deeper into life, open new possibilities of relationship, and accord with the deepest movements of my own soul? If not, then it is toxic, no matter how benign its claim. Does this value, practice, or expectation open me to the mystery of this journey? Jung said in a letter once that life is a short pause between two great mysteries. Beware of those who offer answers. They may be sincere, but their answers are not necessarily yours. Adaptive loyalty to what we have received from our environment may prove an unconscious subversion of the integrity of the soul.

So, to say blandly then, "The choice is yours," is not as simplistic as you may have thought at first. Amid the plethora of voices imposing themselves on you at any moment, which voice amid that cacophony is yours? Which voice rises from the depths of the soul, which from complexes and cultural templates, and how can you know the difference?

This mélange of messages is so profuse. How can we ever choose? And yet, we make choices on a moment-to-moment basis, and not to choose is of course a choice with consequences. So, then the task of this carbonized bit of matter we call our bodies, this tungsten spark we call our soul, is waiting upon us to realize that we serve life when we step forth and begin to take on that responsibility, that accountability, and choose a life that makes sense to us. The choice is ours, and if we are not exercising that choice, someone else is choosing for us—if not the splintered personalities of our complexes, then the perseverating voices of our ancestors, or the noisy din of our cultural tom-toms.

Our life begins twice: the day we are born and the day we accept the radical existential fact that our life, for all its delimiting factors, is essentially ours to choose. And the moment when we open to that invitation and step into that accountability, we take on the power of choice. Perhaps the world as such is meaningless—atoms assembling, disassembling, in a random concatenation of proximities. Perhaps everything is guided by a supreme being whose powers are absolute and whose thought process strikes us at best as arbitrary, surely as inscrutable. Whatever the case, we are the animal that suffers disconnect from meaning. Our system produces a complex series of interactions—feeling responses, dreams ranging from the turbulent and troubling to the transcendent, symptoms, patterns, sudden jolts, insights, recognitions, regressions—and then ineluctably surges forward again and forges new connections. And somewhere in all that complexity is the fantasy of, the possibility of, choice. The argument of whether we are actually free or not goes back into the mists of primal human imagining. But, as Jean Paul Sartre argued, we must act *as if* we are free, take on the "terrible" burden of choice, and be accountable. Whether free or not, we are obliged to act as if we are free, and all systems, philosophies, moralities, and juridical dicta expect accountability.

Years ago a very thoughtful woman who had been raised in a conventional religious setting asked the question that had awakened her at the hour of the wolf: "What if," she said, "Jesus is not divine, not the son of God?" Respectfully, I replied, "What difference does it make?" Of course I knew it meant a great deal of difference to her. But I continued: "You still are accountable for your life. You still have to make choices on a daily basis, and you still are a person who must decide which values, which choices, are worthy of your election."

What stands in the way of the exercise of that power of choice is essentially two things. First, we learned early that trying out who we are in the world often produced negative reactions. So we learned to curb our desires, adapt, perhaps even hide out, and fit in. It is so much safer that way. Tiny in a world of giants, we reason that surely the world is governed by those who know, who understand, who are in control. How disconcerting it is then when we find our own psyches in revolt at these once protective adaptations, and how disillusioning it is to realize that there are very few, if any, adults on the scene who have a clue as to what is going on. Our projections and expectations dissolve in time and are replaced by confusion, dismay, cynicism, and sometimes a frenetic search for trustable authorities.

To say that the choice is ours is both simplistic and profoundly difficult. Sorting through the thicket of admonitions, prohibitions, agendas, and adaptations is neither easy nor common. And yet, each of us has an appointment with ourselves, with our own soul. Whether we keep that appointment and step into the largeness of the summons is another matter. Rilke describes this dilemma in his enigmatic poem "Archaic Torso of Apollo." The speaker in the poem is examining a battered classical sculpture of Apollo. Each crack and crevice is examined, until the examiner gets the uneasy feeling that he too is being examined. He ends by breaking off into a seeming non sequitur: "You must change your life!"

My understanding of Rilke's poem is that once the observer has been in the presence of the large, the timeless, the imaginatively bold, he can no longer be at peace with his own small purchase on life. When we have had our lives reframed and see them as they often are—fear driven, petty, repetitive—we either anesthetize ourselves, distract ourselves, or realize that something has to change. It is usually through numinous moments, as the poet describes, or moments of desperation, or moments when the world gets in our face, forcing us to show up, finally. If we are to show up, we must make choices and stop whining. In those moments, something shifts inside. We experience our life as more fully alive than it has been at any other hour. We realize that we cannot remain bound by fear, convention, or adaptation. We realize that we now have, and have always had, choices. We can say yes or no, but we cannot say we have no choice in the matter.

Can any of us really argue, despite the terrible powers of fate and the impact of others upon our lives, that we are not also the central character in our life drama and that we are making choices every day, whether consciously or not? Can any of us seriously argue that at the end of the journey we have not played some substantial role in the outcome of the journey? Can we continue to argue that our lives are an unfolding novel written from afar, the meaning of which will be revealed to us on the last page only or in some cloudy afterlife? Are we not, on that last page, dead? Are we not writing the script interactively throughout this novel, page by page by page? In the end, are we not impelled to acknowledge the choice is ours, and life waits for us to show up and lay claim to what wishes to be expressed through us?

# Chapter 2

# It's Time to Grow Up

hat does it mean to grow up? Did we not become grown-ups when puberty arrived, when we stepped into large bodies and large agendas? Did we not grow up when we left our familial homes and stepped out into the world and said: "Hire me—I can do that job," "Marry me—I will hold my end of the deal," "Trust me—I can carry that responsibility"? Have we not been grown-ups through responsibly exercising parental, fiduciary, relational, and societal roles for years? And yet, when I have asked people in workshops—reasonable, accomplished, responsible people—"Where do you need to grow up?" why has no one yet asked me to explain that question, why has no one challenged the legitimacy of the assignment, and why has everyone begun writing in a matter of minutes, if not seconds? So, how is it that we play all these mature roles yet know in our heart of hearts that we still have to grow up?

In traditional societies, hanging tenuously to this whirling planet, surviving the onslaught of the elements, harsh conditions, and hostile agencies of all kinds, growing up was a matter of survival. The tribe could not afford to have children idling about. So, without a central committee sending out printed instructions, each civilization evolved rites of passage designed to ensure the transition from the naiveté and dependency of childhood to adult sensibilities that sacrifice comfort and sloth in service to the common interest. After all, social conditions and structures evolve, and technology evolves, but the same human psyche, the same psychodynamics manifest in our ancestors, courses through our current lives. For the bulk of recorded history, we have all had to face the summons to grow up. The difference is that our ancestors were keen observers who understood there is scant motive to sacrifice comfort and dependence unless one is required to do so. So, independently, without a central committee advising them, they came up with something useful: rites of passage.

All passages provide a transition from something that has played out, died, or ceased to be productive. That is what psychotherapy seeks to do in so many cases. Since few, if any, would willingly leave the security of home for the insecure status of adulthood, young people were not asked. They were removed, sometimes forcibly. The six stages of passage varied in form, intensity, duration, and cultural accoutrements, but essentially they were comparable around the world. They involved departure from home, not with an engraved invitation, not with a polite request, but suddenly and decisively. Second, there was a ceremony of death, ranging from being buried in the earth, to immersion, to an effacement of one's known referents. Third, there was a ceremony of rebirth because an emergent being, a differentiated psychology, was dawning. Fourth, they were given the teachings, in three categories: the archetypal stories of the creation, of the gods, of the tribal history; the general roles and polity of adulthood in that culture; and the specific tools of hunting, fishing, child-bearing, and agriculture unique to that tribe. Fifth, there was an ordeal of some kind, often involving isolation in order that one learn to cope with fear and find internal resources. And sixth, after prolonged separation, there was the return to the community as a separated adult. Only in this way did young people transition from the naiveté, dependency, and avoidances of childhood to the expectations of adulthood.

When we examine contemporary culture, we find these rites of passage missing. Instead of tools for personal strength and survival, we teach computer skills. We allow children to abide within the bosom of a protective culture, and accordingly, we have very few initiated, separated, independent persons of adult sensibility. Aging alone does not do it; playing major roles in life does not do it. What is it that shifts one from a needy, blaming, dependent psychology to one of psychospiritual independence? What characterizes our culture better than a needy, whiny clamor for instant gratification, a flight from account-ability, and an inability to tolerate the tension of opposites, rather than learning to live with ambiguity over the long haul and transcending the desire for rapid resolution of life's quiddities?

Life's two biggest threats we carry within: fear and lethargy. Every morning we rise to find two gremlins at the foot of the bed. The one named Fear says, "The world is too big for you, too much. You are not up to it. Find a way to slip-slide away again today." And the one named Lethargy says, "Hey, chill out. You've had a hard day. Turn on the telly, surf the Internet, have some chocolate. Tomorrow's another day." Those perverse twins munch on our souls every day. No matter what we do today, they will turn up again tomorrow. Over time, they usurp more days of our lives than those to which we may lay fair claim. More energy is spent in any given day on managing fear through unre-flective compliance, or avoidance, than any other value. While it is natural to expend energy managing our fears, the magnitude of this effort on a daily basis cannot be overemphasized.

On the other hand, lethargy takes so many seductive forms. We can simply avoid tasks, stay away from what is difficult for us, find ways to numb our days through the thousand soporifics and analgesics the world provides, or possibly worst of all, fall into fundamentalist forms of thinking that finesse subtlety, fuzz opposites, seek simplistic solu-tions to complex issues, and still our spirit's distress with the palliative balm of certainty. Indeed, we have a vast wired culture to help us in this task, a connected twenty-four-hour distraction whose hum both stills anxiety and dims the plaintive cries of our spirit to be served. Drowning in distractions, palliated by simple solutions, and lulled by patronizing authorities, we can sleep our life away and never awaken to the summons of the soul that resounds within each of us.

In *The Eden Project: The Search for the Magical Other*, a book on the psychodynamics of relationships, I noted that all relationships are characterized by two dynamics: *projection* and *transference*. A pro-jection is a mechanism whereby our psychological contents leave us and enter the world seeking an object—a person, an institution, a role—upon which to fasten. Because this occurs unconsciously, we then respond to the other as if we know it, rather than its refracted distortion. Similarly, we transfer to that other—person, institution, role—our personal history in regard to that kind of experience. So, we infantilize our relationships with our intimate other, church, government, organization, or any role that carries presumptive authority with it. In re-evoking our earlier experiences, we unwittingly diminish our adult capacity and present interests by approaching the new moment with avoidant, controlling, or compliant behaviors from our past.

Given the power, the ubiquity, and the subtlety of these projected contents, these transferred historic strategies, we expect others to take care of us, while we cavil against the inadequacies of our affiliations and wonder why our roles alone fail to confirm our maturity and provide continuing satisfaction. From this gap between the expectations of our projections and transferences, we may from time to time come to realize that we are accountable for how things are playing out. When that realization occurs, a heroic summons follows: What am I asking of the other that I am not addressing myself? I suspect that all of us have a sneaking suspicion that we are deferring this question, this responsibility, and have done so for a long time.

I call that question heroic because it embodies a shift in our center of gravity from the other "out there" to the other "within." In other words, something in each of us always knows when we are shirking, avoiding, procrastinating, rationalizing. Sometimes we are obliged to face these uncomfortable facts when our plans, relationships, expectations of others collapse, and we are left holding the bag of consequences. Sometimes others get in our face and demand we deal with what we have avoided. Sometimes we have interruptive symptoms, troubling dreams, meetings with ourselves in dark hours, and then we have to face the fugitive life we are perpetuating. Something within us always knows and always registers its opinion. Naturally, we will avoid this subpoena from the soul as long as we can, until it knocks so forcibly that we have to answer the door. The moment we say, "I am responsible, I am accountable, I have to deal with this," is the day we grow up, at least until the next time, the next regression, the next evasion.

When those attending my workshops so readily begin to write about where they need to grow up, it is not that they haven't thought about it before. Actually, the issues lie quite close to the surface. What has been avoided—a delayed confrontation, the acknowledgment of a talent, a path of reconciliation, or whatever the threatening summons—they have wrestled with many times before. Sadly, what is made conscious does not thereby simply resolve itself. If only it did. The motives for avoidance rise from our existential proclivities to fear and lethargy, and both nemeses win more battles than they lose. All the while, the soul is roiling beneath, sending up protests, distress calls, SOS messages, bills of indictment, and so on. How fast do we have to run and for how long do we have to evade before these bills come home to our living room? Each of us knows all this, which is why it is so relatively simple to acknowledge where we need to grow up.

The hero archetype is an energy we have lauded for millennia: a person who addresses a task, overcomes a fear, acts where needed, and provides an exemplum for others. But do we realize the presence of the hero archetype within us? To call it an archetype is to recognize its universal presence, found in all peoples in all eras. The task of the hero within is to overthrow the powers of darkness, namely, fear and lethargy. All those tales of defeating the dragon are mythopoetic versions of overthrowing the power of that which would swallow us, as both fear and lethargy do on a daily basis. Sooner or later, we are each called to face what we fear, respond to our summons to show up, and overcome the vast lethargic powers within us. This is what is asked of us, to show up as the person we really are, as best we can manage, under circumstances over which we may have no control. This showing up as best we can is growing up. That is all that life really asks of us: to show up as best we can.

I have always been moved by the example of Marcus Aurelius. Though he was the emperor and could have enjoyed any besotted sinecure back in Rome, he chose to be out in the field to face the Hun who wished to kill him. Was he different from us? No, he had the same fears and lethargic impulses we all have. Every day was a battle for him, as it is for us. He was as susceptible as we to the easy comfort of despair that we have more to handle than someone else or that others are better equipped than we for life's journey. All of us have the same fears, the same seductive lethargy, and the same capacity for avoiding growing up. To compensate for my intimidation by fear and my inducement to lethargic avoidance, I often read the words of Marcus Aurelius as he rose in the morning, full of doubt, flush with fear, and replete with ready rationalizations to avoid what threatened:

> At day's first light, have in readiness, against disinclination
> to leave your bed, the thought that "I am rising for the
> work of man." Must I grumble at setting out to do what
> I was born for, and for the sake of which I have been
> brought into the world? Is this the purpose of my creation,
> to lie here under the blankets and keep myself warm? "Ah,
> but it is a great deal more pleasant!" Was it for pleasure,
> then, that you were born and not for work?[1]

When I read these words to myself, I imagine I can see him, sharing the fate of his comrades, cold and shivering on the freezing Donau, and facing implacable enemies. And why do I repeatedly read these words? Because they remind me to stop feeling sorry for myself, my privileged life and privileged opportunities, and to stop whining and looking for an easy path. I remind myself to show up, in the best way I can, winning some of those internal battles against fear and lethargy, losing some, but with the fond hope that if I show up as best I can, then I will also be a grown-up. That is what life asks of each of us: to grow up, be accountable, be present. That is what our partners ask of us, our children ask of us, and our world asks of us. When we show up as best we can, then on any given day, we are a grown-up and contribute to carrying the world's burden, rather than adding to it.

Ask yourself these simple questions: Where do I need to grow up, step into my life? What fear will I need to confront in doing so? Is that fear realistic or from an earlier time in my development? And, given that heavy feeling I have carried for so long already, what is the price I have to pay for not growing up?

# Chapter 3

# Let Go of the Old

In Albert Camus's short story "The Guest," he depicts a man who wishes to avoid all responsibility. Set in Algeria at the time of the revolution against the colonial authorities, a young schoolteacher aligns with neither side, and when he is charged with holding a rebel until the authorities arrive, he gives the prisoner the opportunity to escape, pointing out the path to the freedom of the desert versus captivity in the colonial prison. When he sees that his prisoner has taken the chance to slip away the next morning, he feels free from consequences only to find out that his prisoner has chosen the path to incarceration instead of freedom and that he himself is now the target of the retributive wrath of the revolutionaries. So there is within the lives of all of us the frequent choice to remain within the predictable, the safe, the familiar, even the miserable, thinking it preferable to the uncertainty of the unknown. How often do we look back "longing for the freedom of our chains," rather than stepping into the opening maw of uncertainty?

Freud identified what he called "the repetition compulsion," the drive within us to replicate the old, even if it is painful and leads us to predictable but familiar dead ends. First, we can acknowledge the power of negative programming in our lives. The examples are plentiful. How many abused children seek out, even marry, abusers? How many abusers repeat their pathologically circumscribed images of relationship? But Freud also speculated that one might repeat the traumatizing experience as somehow "safer" than the original, believing somehow that it will be better this time. So, the prisoner chooses prison rather than the abyss of open choices, the desert of unlimited freedoms. The schoolteacher "chooses" not to choose, apparently to avoid the consequences of choice, and the watchful gods bring upon him the terrible consequences of that choice.

Letting go of the old is apparently much more difficult than we think. We believe we do so by redecorating our homes, taking a different kind of vacation, even swapping relational partners, but the replicative patterns remain. The only constant presence in every scene of that long-running soap opera we call our life is us. So, undeniably, we have to bear responsibility for how this story is unfolding. And yet, why do these patterns, especially those that are harmful to us and others, have such a grip on us?

Where we find patterns, we also will likely find core, emotion-laden ideas within us, ideas that may or may not be conscious, may or may not be accurate, may not even be ours but have been part of our formative experience and the primal atmosphere we inhabited. We all internalize messages from daily life—from popular media; from our family of origin; from religious, educational, political, economic, and other cultural influences; and from the vagaries of our personal biographies. These messages tell us what to do: avoid this, engage that, perform this action; or they instruct us what not to do: be quiet, hide out, don't reveal what you are feeling. We were not born with these messages, but we have them because we have a history and because we are sensitive beings in need of "reading" the world around us to serve our survival, get our needs met as best we can, and fit in.

Given that the most powerful and the least considered messages derive from our earliest experiences of safety, peril, and adaptive instructions, whenever they are activated in our psychic life, they have the power to usurp consciousness, take over, and execute their archaic programs. The most powerful of these messages derive from our earliest relationships and tend to accumulate as a series of reflexive responses to the stimuli of life. While they were once phenomenological, namely experiential and not conscious, over time they become "institutionalized" responses to the tasks, troubles, and turbulence of the world. No wonder we have patterns. Letting go of them proves the most difficult of our tasks because they once were, and sometimes remain, tied to our survival, our fitting in, our acceptance by others.

Old loyalties, old understandings, old commitments may very well have bound our days together in predictable ways, but these same constructs can also bind us to a disabling past or a limiting view of others. The nature of our psyche is based on change, growth, curiosity, and imagination. But there are very conservative elements within us that retain a commitment to the known, the familiar, even when it is based on constrictive perspectives. Look at the discord in our nation in the face of social evolution, change, and erosion of the old "certainties." When I was a child, the presumptive fixities of gender role and definition; racial, ethnic, and sexual practices; and ethical categories were presumed to be given by the gods, ordained by unchallenged scriptures or venerated institutions. There is not one of these "fixities" whose ontological claim has not been deconstructed. Never in human history have individuals been freer to choose their life path, their values, and to serve what is true for them. And with this freedom comes a tremendous backlash that opportunistic politicians utilize to their advantage. Those who want the "good old days," who "want their country back," are really wishing (a) that their once-privileged position be ratified and reified and (b) that the anxiety of ambiguity be treated with the anodyne of "certainty," "received authority," and "traditional values." What is not addressed—indeed what is most exploited, in every country, every culture, every religious or political hegemony under the onslaught of change—is how much of the blowback is fueled by human psychopathology. That is, how much cultural tension, conflict, and frenzy arise out of the anxiety of change, of ambiguity, of evolution, of eroded "certainties." Little do such groups realize that their normative stories are just that: stories, interpretations, which were once repressed and resented as they, too, overthrew the certainties of their age. As well, our present culture wars will be viewed by succeeding eras as laughably archaic, uninformed, and constrictive.

Former Illinois governor and US ambassador to the United Nations Adlai Stevenson once observed that the moral measure of a nation is how it treats its least advantaged citizens. So, too, we may add a corollary: the moral measure of a culture is found in the degree to which individuals and groups can tolerate ambiguity and change and how open they can be to the otherness of others. By that definition, this modern world is not doing very well. But are there values worth preserving? Of course there are: decency, toleration, respect for others. Right now, I am betting on human psychopathology to prevail, as it most often does, even though I work on the one person I can work on, myself, to try to render myself more amenable to creative living in the presence of change, ambiguity, and the erosion of those old certainties.

So, letting go of the old is not easy. It requires being able to tolerate the aroused level of anxiety that besets any of us when ego consciousness is not in control. It requires that we let go of what we thought certain and cast our lifeboats upon a tenebrous sea. The more we resist change, the more we are allied against the nature of nature and the developmental agenda of our own psyches. Being aligned against our own nature is the very definition of neurosis. One obvious, but perhaps unconscious, example of this resistance is found in our culture's obsession with and denial of aging and mortality, the natural, evolving process within our body and our soul that is programmed in our DNA and begins unfolding from our first moment of life. How many times have people hung on to their youth, resisted growth and graceful accommodation with nature "naturing" within them? Facing his own aging, ailing, and mortal process, Yeats wrote in "Sailing to Byzantium" that the soul is obliged to "sing, and louder sing, for every tatter in its mortal dress." In other words, for every outer diminishment, we are tasked with a summons to larger engagement with the soul within. This process alone brings us meaning, growth, and the resilience of the spirit; the alternative is a continuously fugitive life.

Life is a series of attachment and losses, beginning with our disconnect from the womb, a primal trauma from which we never wholly recover. During our journey, we link with, attach to, and also separate from others on a continuing basis. People come and go in our lives. Some of these losses are traumatic: a marriage that sinks, a child lost, a career up in smoke. These things hurt, yet not to move forward in service to life, in service to bringing more into this world, is to abrogate our reason for being here—to bring our more evolved chip to the great mosaic of being, a humbling and ennobling participation in the vast puzzle that the human venture has been adding to or subtracting from since its beginning in the African veldt many millennia ago.

Attachment and loss, attachment and loss—this is the human story. We lose parts of ourselves as we adapt to the demands of the world. Those for whom we care are often lost through death, divorce, or dysfunction. Whether we absorb those losses into our system and soldier on or remain stuck at the level of the loss is the question. For example, those who have experienced betrayal in their lives often remain attached to the wound and the implicit message of that experience. I cannot number those whom I have seen who are still hanging on to an earlier image of themselves, moments of weakness, self-betrayal, or failure, who sustain their attachment to an earlier self-image rather than learn from it and move on. And how many choose people in their lives who will repeat that pattern for them? The woman who selects loser after loser because she was never sure her father was there for her and through all this repetition compulsion blames herself, thinking, as every child does, "I am what happened to me. I am my experience. If I were worthy of love, he would have been there for me." Her ghostly father imago gets transferred to inappropriate man after inappropriate man. And the man who feels dependent upon the woman but distances himself from her because he fears the magnitude of his own need reads her reactions to his distancing as a confirmation of her ill intentions toward him from the beginning. All of these common relational patterns in our lives arise because we are still attached to our earliest experiences of self and other. All of these patterns arise from a driving idea, with its attendant message, the defining stories fate provides us. Until we realize that we are still in relationship to that complex, that intrapsychic imago of self and other, we are doomed like the ancient mariner to wander with our repetitive story.

Letting go of the old is infinitely more difficult than we think. How difficult it is to grasp the wisdom of Samuel Beckett in *Endgame*: "play and lose, and have done with losing." We have been defined by our history, our attachments, our provisional definitions of ourselves and others, and we cling to our history with tenacity precisely because to think of ourselves in other ways is either intimidating or unimaginable. But the human psyche imagines more. The problem with complexes is that they have no imagination. They can only say over and over the phenomenological message of their origins. But the psyche has a much larger perspective on our lives. It imagines much more for us than the ordinary ego can comprehend.

Ironically, psychopathology is one of the signs of the larger imagination of the psyche, or soul. If we had no soul, that is, had no organ of meaning, our adaptations would be our reality. But the soul protests and registers its protest through our body, our troubling dreams, our affective invasions, such as depression or our addictive, anesthetizing self-treatment. While most of modern psychiatry and psychotherapy prefer to work around these protests and thereby drive the internal conflict deeper, the psychodynamic understanding of symptoms, dreams, and behavioral patterns is rather to ask: Why have you come? What is it you are protesting? What is the desire of the soul (as opposed to the desires of my environment, my complexes, my history)? These questions do not bury the issue, try to bypass it, or medicate it into numbness, but rather approach the soul with dignity and ask, as we might of any stranger who knocks unbidden at our door, "Why have you come? What do you want? How might we converse?"

Only with this sort of respect for the dialogue with the psyche can we begin to leave the old behind. Much in our history is worthy of carrying forward, and much is not. Just as we periodically clean the house, go through old clothes and fashions and discard the no longer germane, so we have to go through our accumulated histories, our driving attitudes, reflexes, and responses, and discard what is no longer useful, productive, relevant, or serving growth. As Saint Paul writes in his Letter to the Corinthians, when we become adults, it is time to put away childish things. Only then may we lay claim to our cooperative journeys into that unknown, which is asking us to be brave, thoughtful, and courageous.

# Chapter 4

# Recover Personal Authority

In *Shambhala: The Sacred Path of the Warrior*, Chögyam Trungpa defines the warrior not as an agent of destruction but as one who is "brave," and then observes "that this is the definition of bravery: not being afraid of yourself."[1] This is an incredible paradox. Why should we be afraid of ourselves? We weren't born that way. But soon we learn experientially, and increasingly consciously, that we are tiny, vulnerable, and dependent upon the huge powers around us, most notably the giants we later call parents. Whatever powers nature invested in us are easily overrun by the forces outside of us, and so we learn to deny, even fear, the powers within.

For example, Cynthia spends her life feeling inadequate and ill equipped for her life. Her patterns are a combination of avoidance, timorous responses to challenges, and even self-sabotage. She had the fortune/misfortune to be the child of a star, a highly accomplished, highly degreed, highly recognized mother, whom she believed she was called to emulate. Whatever capacities she may or may not have been granted by the fates, Cynthia believed early on that she was incapable of meeting the level of her mother's achievements. No one, apparently, explained to her that she wasn't supposed to equal or surpass her mother because that would have been living her mother's life and not her own.

How many of us have felt compelled to look over our shoulder and compare ourselves with classmates, neighbors, or ancestors, and believe that we have to equal whatever they did in their lives? What few of us know is that many whom we would emulate have (if we were to experience their inner reality) served demonic self-doubt and self-recrimination, and frequently with drives that pathologized them even as they garnered accolades. Few of us realize that *it is not what we do but what we are in service to inside that makes all the difference.* If we but knew what drove, hounded, and compelled those whom we admire, we might truly not want to live their lives after all.

Jung asserted that all our difficulties derive from the fact that we become separated from our instincts, those internal energies, drives, and feeling states that move us toward greater wholeness. And Nietzsche further characterized us as "the sick animal." Neither was, of course, endorsing a life governed only by instinctual impulse, but the suspicion of, the fear of, and the estrangement from those instincts mean that one is cut off from the vital, nourishing roots of life. Too much instinct constricts us to an animal existence, but too much consciousness separates us from our natural sources.

The first half of life, at least for most of us, is essentially a giant, unavoidable mistake. When I have offered this thought, with deliberate hyperbole, to various audiences, inevitably people laugh, the laugh of rueful recognition. When well-meaning parents have asked, "What can I do to spare my child the disappointments and disasters of life?" I have said, "You can do little, if anything, because they have to try out their lives, make those mistakes, and learn whatever they can from them." In time, such painful experience becomes the smithy in which a more authentic journey becomes possible—that is, if one does the work to learn what there is to learn.

The second half of life is not a chronological moment but a psychological moment that some people, however old, however accomplished, however self-satisfied in life, never reach. The second half of life occurs when people, for whatever reason—death of partner, end of marriage, illness, retirement, whatever—are obliged to radically consider who they are apart from their history, their roles, and their commitments. Every young person "escapes" home and then goes out to repeat it, to be owned by it in overcompensation, or to attempt to "treat" it unconsciously through an addiction, a fugitive life, or some form of distraction. Given that the farther away one gets from those primal influences, the more these spectral influences still call the shots, most people sooner or later hit a wall. What they do then makes all the difference in their life.

A thoughtful, conscientious, accomplished life that ends prematurely may mean simply that that person served the complexes, tapes, instructions, or fears of his or her family, or *Sitz im Leben* (a German phrase, roughly translated as "setting in life"). It is only when fate or something very deep within forces us to examine our essential premises that we ever begin to consider, and possibly differentiate, the streams of influence that flow within us.

We have to recover personal authority because the din and demand of the world is too huge to ignore, too intrusive to resist, even if we think we have rebelled and held to our own course. And yet, every time someone avers, "I haven't lived my mother's life," or "I won't repeat my father's path," they are still responding to someone else's life, some de facto external authority. At any given moment our ego consciousness is subject to a plethora of voices, a cacophony of claims upon it. Which voices are mine? Which admonitions derive from another time or place? We don't often ask those questions. Finding personal authority requires two things: sorting through the traffic within and living what we find with courage and consistency. In a letter in the 1950s, Jung observed that the work of being an evolved human being consists of three parts. Psychology can bring us *insight*, but then, he insisted, come the moral qualities of the individual: *courage* and *endurance*. So, having potentially come to consciousness, to have embraced insight as to what a dilemma is really about, one then has to find the courage to live it in the real world, with all its punitive powers, and to do so over time in the face of opposition both external and internal.

The failure to understand this triune task—insight, courage, endurance—leads many to misunderstand the dilemmas we face in life. Thus the couple that approaches a marriage counselor to "work on their relationship" may not have discerned what forces, healthy or unhealthy, brought them together in the first place and what it means to "stick to a commitment." In one person's history, conflict may have been so invasive that she will cut and run at the first opportunity, and therefore that person's summons in the relationship has little to do with the outer partnership but a great deal to do with confronting the fears of history and the compelling defenses of flight. The other person may have learned helplessness in early childhood, where a reticulated overpowering environment said, "You have no rights here; you have no choices here." Such an individual will remain in bondage to a narcissistic partner, an abusive other, who simply repeats the pathologizing messages of history. If that person is to see that his "enemy" in this context is not the partner but the compelling powers of conditioning history, then he may realize that longevity alone is an unworthy goal. It is not the other, but our relationship to history, to the disabling messages of our dependent past, that is imprisoning. Again, simply to realize this is only part of the battle. Then comes the courage to face what is internally programmed and still feels terrifying—the disapproval, the anger, the putative retaliation of the other. Ninety percent of the fears that bind us derive from our psychological history, when adaptation, surrender of personal truth, was obliged by an environmental situation. Not only is this archaic anxiety to be confronted in the moment of insight, but over time, day in and day out, the rest of our life. It sounds simple perhaps in the telling, but going through our historic fears of overwhelmment or abandonment is the hardest thing we ever have to do. And we have to do it today, here, now, and again tomorrow, to ever recover personal authority.

So, to come back to that telling definition of bravery—not to be afraid of oneself—we see that we are all asked to re-vision our journey, to reframe our understanding of self and world. Ironically, we are abetted in this process by something called *psychopathology*. This is a rather ugly word, but etymologically it translates as "an expression of the suffering of a soul." That translation puts a different spin on things surely. It could be argued that life is actually rather simple. If you do what is right for you, it is right for you; if you do what is wrong for you, it is wrong for you. But it is not so simple, is it?

How do we know what is right for us? Well, the body knows, our deepest feeling knows, and the psyche knows, and each expresses its opinion, even as we learned early in life to evade these continuous messages from our own depths. So, the recovery effort must typically begin with the experience of inner discord, outer conflict, and sometimes heartache and loss.

Whatever health and wholeness is, it surely involves aligning our outer choices with our inner reality. When the path we are on is right for our souls, the energy is there. When what we are doing is wrong for us, we can temporarily mobilize energy in service to goals, and often we must, but in time such forced mobilization leads to irritability, anger, burnout, and symptoms of all kinds. When what we are doing is right for us, the feeling function supports us. That is, our autonomous feeling system supports rather than opposes our choices. The support of this autonomous evaluative process confirms the rightness of our choices, even when those around us do not endorse them. When we are doing what is right for us, we will feel a sense of purpose, meaning, and satisfaction, and that communicates itself to others also.

Living our personal authority will not spare us from conflict, from suffering, from marginalization, or even from martyrdom. Many whom we most admire in history lived wretched lives, but we venerate them because something truthful was served through them. They lived their calling in the way in which we all are called.

Sorting and sifting over time leads to *discernment*. That is what is necessary to find our voice in the midst of the many claims upon us, the collisions of obligations, and the impulsive service to our complexes. And then, as Jung reminded, come the moral qualities. Can I mobilize the courage to face my life, to meet all the challenges that show up, knowing that I am most undermined by the adaptive reflexes within that were once so necessary? Those "protections" are now constrictions in which I am imprisoned by my own past. And then can I live those choices out over time, in the face of consequences, perhaps the loss of understanding and support of loved ones or estrangement from my tribe? Sometimes we simply have to set out on that course because we are inescapably aware of our life as a summons to show up as ourselves, as best we can. Sometimes we have to act as if we are not afraid simply not to be governed by fear. In those moments, we move from creatures of adaptation to creatures whose lives testify to the unfolding possibilities of being.

Insight, courage, and endurance—not a bad litany of which to be mindful every day. The days we remember and do our best—all that is ever asked of us—are the days in which we reclaim personal authority from the vaults of history. Then we may know we have truly moved into the second half of life, the part where we get our life back.

# Chapter 5

# Seek to Make Amends

Most of us are aware of the ninth step of recovery programs: to make amends to those whom we have harmed, where doing so would not produce further harm. Again, this sounds simple and is clearly the right thing to do, when we can. But is it so simple?

The easy part, as it is not easy, is to come to an awareness of how our narcissism, our self-interest, our selfishness, our ignorance, or our unconsciousness has brought harm to others. This difficulty certainly applies to members of groups, such as nations, institutional organizations, and political, social, and economic movements that overtly or indirectly have brought harm to others. Those of us cast by fate into so-called first-world nations have long lived on the back of the disadvantaged. Upon whose back have our comforts, our clothing, our shoes, our products, our lifestyle come? Whose continued exploitation will our lives demand? These are not easy questions, and if we dare answer them, what then? Do we harden the heart one more time, find the ready rationalization, and distract ourselves as before? And how do we make amends to generations of indigenous peoples, whose civilizations were destroyed in the name of our "progress"? How do we compensate ethnic groups suppressed and oppressed by the juggernaut of history that privileges one group at the cost of another? Making amends must start, then, with a greater awareness of the sins of our ancestors, how we have been privileged by those injustices, and how that injustice is perpetuated by unconsciousness, indifference, rationalized self-interest, and sheer momentum to this present day.

Making amends to those whom we have personally hurt, through our actions or inactions, is also difficult, for it requires us to become conscious first of all. In *Swamplands of the Soul*, I examined three levels of guilt: contextual guilt, direct guilt, and inauthentic guilt. Contextual guilt is described in the paragraph above. No nation has come to power without oppressing some of its citizens, no economic system represents a level playing field, and no exceptionalism is free of rationalized injustices. Those who argue otherwise are morally obtuse or overtly evil, for much evil arises from such indifferent worship of self-interest.

There is, of course, the guilt that arises from an honest reckoning with ourselves, the face we have to confront every morning in the mirror as we brush our teeth—direct guilt. There is no adult on the planet from whom a long line of consequences does not trail. Sometimes those consequences are brought to consciousness by someone telling us how we have hurt them, neglected them, ignored them, imposed our needs upon them, and so on. Such an accounting can bring a crippling guilt, understandable perhaps, but serving no one, certainly not the ones injured already.

Again, where possible, recompense may be redemptive, restorative; however, life seldom allows us a second chance at these matters. And many have spent their days trying to work off smudged karma they believe they have accumulated in thoughtless hours. Sometimes this legitimate accountability may be compensated in symbolic ways through the enactment of compensatory acts. Such enactment, however, must come consciously lest the person be ensnared in the foul nets of compulsivity one more time. It does matter whether we serve something redemptive or something demonic. And it matters even more that we discern the origins of whatever we do and whether doing so serves something healing in us or something that binds us in new ways to the disabling past.

The incapacity to feel this sort of honest guilt marks either the narcissist, who is too weak to take on the burden of his or her choices, or the sociopath, in whom the capacity for relatedness shut down many years before. For most of us, the pragmatic question always remains, What does my honest guilt make me do or keep me from doing?

The third form of guilt, inauthentic guilt, rises from a misnomer: we are not guilty; we are anxious. Most of us learned early that enacting who we are was not particularly welcome, was even risky, so we learned to split from our own nature and did so long enough to lose contact with it. In each of us there is a protective monitor. When a natural impulse arises, a spontaneous motive or act, some old, archaic warning system is also alerted and shuts it down. So, people who perfectly understand that the power to say yes or no to a moment constitutes the essential freedom and dignity of every soul will also say, "And I feel guilty when I say no." Why are we guilty? Guilty of what? The legitimacy of our own nature? Why have we learned to ally so strongly against ourselves? I am describing an internal protective system whose roots are in our archaic past, whose purpose is to take care of us, but which undermines our truth, our integrity, our adulthood. This protection we may label guilt, but it is really about anxiety management.

With each of these "swampland" encounters, there is a task, the identification of which, and the engagement with which, can lead to enlargement. When, for example, we feel guilty, we can submit the feeling state to a simple test. Is it harm I have brought to another, whether intended or not? Or is it some form of inner split, in which I ally against my own reality in service to fitting in or avoiding retribution of one kind or another, and therefore continuously undermining the possibility of this moment with the protective programs of the past?

If we find the third guilt, the protective mechanism in its familiar play, then renewed intentionality is demanded. In the end, we can address these self-imposed constrictions in only one way: counterphobic behavior. That's right: we have to do what we are afraid of. Everything that this guilt is protecting must be experienced. Only then, when the old anxiety washes over us and then recedes, can we stand there as ourselves. Only when we can go through this wave of anxiety, and find that it does not destroy, defeat, deter, or divert us, can we learn to be free of it.

For all the amends we owe this broken world, for all the recompense we owe others, we also owe ourselves permission to be who we really are, finally, before we are no longer here. We have to make amends to our soul for all the moments of complicity, cowardice, and co-optation that were once protective but now sour the soul and render it bitter.

# Chapter 6

# Step Out from under
# the Parental Shade

Our first models of the "other" derive from our immediate caregivers. What we know now, we could not know then. Parents are not giants, though their bodies appear huge. Parents are not gods, though they seem authoritative enough. Parents are not all knowing, though we suspect they read our minds rather easily. Only later do we begin to realize they were just people like us, often with histories that we little know, with scant access to the literature, the information, and the media we take for granted. What they learned about life, the instructions they got, usually came from their models, the exigencies of their time, minus the range of permission most of us have today to examine, compare notes, and critique everything with the latest information. Most of them walked in ignorance and fear and with inordinate pressures—all without the opportunity to express themselves that we take for granted. Their lives were often furtive, secretive, guilt ridden, and silent, for to speak of these matters was to risk large consequences. Those of other religions or races were suspect. Though they professed goodwill toward all, they were also afraid of otherness and clung to stereotypes and traditional lines of constricted exposure and communication. It was not a world for which nostalgia is appropriate. There are no "good old days." Memory is deceptive, and what is longed for is that unconsciousness, that "certainty" that comforted the ignorant and kept them safe within their fixed categories of belief and behavior. It was a constrictive world, an ignorant, fear-bound, prejudicial, and bigoted world, and I am grateful so much of it is gone.

In the face of such large examples, such overt and covert instructions, we have three choices: repeat what we saw, serve the messages; run from them into overcompensation; or try to "fix the problem," heal the split within in any way, little knowing what gave rise to and sustains that split within us.

Most commonly we serve the model, the instructions, the stuck places we experienced in our families of origin, churches, synagogues, mosques, and neighborhoods. All children desperately need some security, some reassurance, and what is more secure than common values, common practices, common prohibitions, common marching orders, and common expectations to meet? Only if we make the mistake of travel and find that there is another world, another set of choices over that hill, do we tumble into a larger world of possibilities. And so the stifling patterns roll over into the next generation until, as in the ancient Greek tragic trilogies, some person suffers enough, comes to consciousness enough, and breaks the skein of cause and effect. Only when the incestuous values of tribalism—the most emotionally seductive but psychologically primitive, culturally impoverished, and dangerous idea of all—are transcended does renewal ever come to the person or the group.

Second, something in us sounds an alarm, announcing: "Something is wrong here; this is not right for you. You must find a better way." Most children try at least once, and most get slapped down or find the isolation or punishment too much to bear. Most children go underground. Some act out in ways inexplicable to themselves or others, while a few have the courage to break forth and declare their independence, no matter what the cost.

Such persons, sensing the difficulty of replicating someone else's life, even that of a beloved parent, understand that "I cannot live my mother's life," or "I won't repeat my father's life." And, with the best of intentions, they choose a partner to replace the parent or one whose values repudiate the parent's, and so on. Overcompensation is still being governed by the "not that," rather than from some guiding energy within.

Or third, the person lives an ongoing "treatment plan," a life constructed on blotting out, fixing, avoiding, and resolving those primal models and instructions. We have a popular culture, after all, whose chief purpose is distraction. But distraction from what? The existential yawn of the abyss? The progressive unfolding of aging, debilitation, and death? The deep anguish of the soul that has lost its way? Yes, all of these, and more. Distraction means we can stay wired to the Internet, entertainment, conversation, controversy, and seductive images and ideologies, and therefore no longer dwell in the house of remembrance. Or we can live a life of numbing—excessive work, drugs and alcohol, directive ideologies, compelling causes—allowing us to override the still voice of the soul within.

I do not mean to suggest that all parenting is pathogenic. Quite the contrary, most parents mean well and do their best, as characterized by even the generation of parents with whom I grew up. I never faulted their good intentions or love for me, and to this day I grieve how much it cost them and what deformations of their own souls they suffered, about which they seldom complained. After all, they grew up not expecting much more than struggle, hardship, and, at best, to be thought well of by their peers. There are bad people and really bad parents, but these were not bad people or bad parents. Jung's comment that the largest burden the child must bear is the unlived life of the parent is a stunning reminder of the silent cost these generations bore. Jung's own father was chronically depressed and unable to question the premises of his belief, his conditioning, or his tribe; his mother was chronically unstable. And so, Jung confessed, when he thought of father, the word "powerless" came to mind, and when he thought of mother, the word "unreliable" came to his mind. So, set forth into the world with the dynamos of powerlessness and unreliability in your engine room, either you repeat it, overcompensate for it, or try to fix it.

The first half of life is characterized by the role these influences play in our lives. We leave home believing we have left our parents behind and step into large roles, large decisions, and most of all, large accountabilities as we become parents ourselves. We are struggling to find our own ways, thinking we have left that family of origin, that tribalism, behind.

But given the power of such idealized images, we serve them, try to make up for them, or seek unconsciously to fix them. And therein the next generation receives the imprint not only of us but also of the often-invisible generations that preceded it. Only through suffering, coming to consciousness, and being humbled, can one start anew.

When we violate our psyches, our souls, the moment does not go unrecognized by something within. So often the task of the therapist is to receive these reports, dilemmas, and recast them into another perspective. Then one learns that the psychic protests, the relational discords, and the generalized dis-ease have meaning after all. The forty-year-old woman who is gifted with a dream that she is in the hospital, visited by her favorite relative, and told she is going to die, is not afflicted with a terminal illness. Rather, she is being told by a helpful agency within her that the premises, scripts, and roles of the first half of her life have been served, and something else is about to begin. In the reframing of that dream, and so many other symptomatic portraits, one can move from the psychopathology of the hour toward meaning. So rather than repress the symptom, anesthetize the discord it causes, we might rather ask: Why has it come? What is it asking of me? And in light of this portrait from the interior, how might I re-vision my life? Only in these moments do we begin to move out from under the influence, however well intended, of the parental conceptions, paradigms, limitations, and models.

Through the years, so many conscientious parents have asked me, "How can I spare my children this discord through which I have had to pass?" My answer has always been something of a disappointment to them. The one thing parents can do for their children is live their lives as fully as they can, for this will open the children's imagination, grant permission to them to have their own journey, and open the doors of possibility for them. Wherever we are stuck, they will have a tendency to be stuck also or will spend their life trying to overcompensate. Living our own journey as fully as possible is not only a gift to our soul, it also frees up the generation behind us to live theirs as well. The very freedom to live our lives that we wished from our parents, we thereby grant to our children to live theirs.

# Chapter 7

# Vow to Get Unstuck

Through the years, a question that I often ask in workshops around the world is "Where are you stuck?" Inevitably, in every workshop, wherever given, there are questions about the questions: "What does this mean?" "Can you give an example?" "Is this all right?" These questions are understandable at one level, but at another, they are symptomatic of the unstated problem of personal authority: Is this what you want, and therefore I will have your approval? Can I do this? And what happens if I guess incorrectly? The presumption is that of the parent-child template no matter how much we contend otherwise. I write this not in judgment or criticism but merely to point out how subtle, how systemic, the template of external authority is, how it persists even in the most productive of lives, and how stuck one may be even around the question "Where are you stuck?"

Still, in all those occasions and geographies, never has anyone asked me to define what I mean by *stuck*, even when the word is translated into Swedish, Russian, or Portuguese. And everyone starts writing in their journal within one to two minutes, suggesting that the concept of stuckness is quite close to the surface in our lives and that we all have a sense of where we are stuck. But if we find it so easy to bring to mind our stuckness, why is it so difficult to get unstuck?

For millennia, humans have recognized that we are often our own worst enemies, that the same problems show up again and again in our lives. In his Letter to the Romans, Paul observes that though he knows the good, he does not often do it. Why? He employs a Greek word, *akrasia*, which might be translated as a "dilatory will," or an insufficiency of intention. Why then—if these stuck places hurt us, embarrass us, and perhaps even spill over onto others—don't we will more, will better, be more resolved?

We may be sure that wherever there is a stuck place in our life, we have a sore toe from stubbing it, and that a complex has built up around this contentious, tender place. We can, of course, mobilize even more will, which sometimes proves effective, and the obstacle is pushed through. But most of the time, renewed, ever-persistent stuckness prevails.

I suggest two principles of depth psychology that might be useful here. By *depth psychology*, I mean to take into account the whole person, not just the externalized behavior. I propose to dialogue with the unconscious world (an impossibility from the perspective of limited consciousness), to track the invisible energies that course through the venues of the visible. To that end then, two principles:

It's not about what it's about.

What you see is a compensation for what you don't see.

The first principle tells us that the place of stuckness is not about what it appears to be about. So what then is it about? For example, a common resolve, so easily frustrated, is the desire to lose weight, exercise more, or practice other self-improvement behaviors. But why do these intentions get set so easily aside?

Much of eating, to choose one example, is driven by invisible agendas, the nutritive needs of the psyche, the hungers of the flesh and spirit. The more concrete the need, the more easily understood. The more abstract, the more elusive. If food were just about food, then we could measure the amounts and count the calories rather easily. But food is animated matter. And matter derives from the *Mater*. What feeds our needs most deeply? We project onto the raw material of food our emotional and social needs, far in addition to the nutritional needs of the organism. Food becomes love, continuity, ready presence. No matter how miserable the day, we can come home, open the fridge, and "lights on, and welcome home!" And why is it we have so many eating disorders—anorexia, bulimia, obesity? These disorders are hypermanagement efforts in a world elsewhere beyond our control or a plaintive cry that there is never enough love, security, or reassurance. Why not? When the life of the spirit is compromised by the decline of the mediatorial institutions and connective imagery to the transcendent, one transfers the search for the numinous—that which speaks to the soul, engages the spirit—to some surrogate such as power, business, sex, satiety, or a palliative substance.

So, how difficult it then becomes to regulate by will alone these metaphor-carrying, symbol-embodying substances. We think it's about food alone, sustenance alone, but it is about all that is missing in our life—and why would we let go of our available anodyne, our treatment plan? That is where the stuckness originates and then grows armored with Maginot Lines of defense, rationalization, and reinforcements. So, we have to analyze what the stuck place is really about. Also, we need to recognize that what we are readily able to identify, the behavior, for example, is only what is visible, while it is the invisible mechanism that runs our lives.

Under each stuck place there is a wire, so to speak, that reaches down into the archaic field and activates a field of anxiety of which we are largely unaware but that has enough power to reinforce whatever complex has been holding the line against change. As anxiety, it is amorphous, free-floating, imperceptible, yet quite real. If we can reach into that obscuring cloud, we might find specific fears. To give an example, if I let go of my daily connection to the food as a reassuring object, what then will be there in the darkness for me? I recall a woman in a bad relationship saying to me that she would not let go of that hand until there was another hand in the darkness for her. So we cling to that which in the end offers only a modicum of nurturance and leaves behind its traces in the corpulent body. So too of sexual dependency, ritualized behaviors, and all that seems to offer continuity and connection in a disjunctive world. What numinous links were once provided for many through tribal mythology are presently scattered amid the secular world, where individuals now must search for their own connections.

In the end, there are two existential threats to our survival and well-being: the fear of *overwhelmment* and the fear of *abandonment*. In the encounter with the former, we are reminded of our relative powerlessness in a large and potentially invasive world. This discrepancy, this unpredictability of the environment, is inculcated in childhood, reinforced and ratified by multiple experiences of the power of the world over our capacities. No wonder so many power stratagems show up in intimate relationships, for who does not want to stake out something measurable, predictable, and controllable.

Similarly, the opposite existential threat, abandonment, means the person is driven to achievement in order to attain the reassuring accolades of the other, or transfers the need for nurturance, constancy, or reassurance to some promising surrogate yet estranges the other through coercive behaviors. The person might also seek a position in life wherein approval and reassurance are structurally provided, or become addicted to a substance whose presence is easily managed yet whose payoff in satisfaction progressively declines. This need to connect to, hold fast to, and fixate the other is one of our most common human patterns in reacting to change, discontinuity, and ambiguity.

It is for this reason that fundamentalisms of all kinds, in all corners of the world, respond to the changes in our time, the deconstruction of presumed fixities, with so much militancy and even violence. Those same troubled souls would not insist on the medicine practiced millennia ago were they to visit the ER of their hospitals tonight, yet they insist on tribal, agrarian, and parochial dogmas ratified by tradition in their tribal histories, with all of their primitive rules and prejudices. All of this disparate and desperate behavior is a reaction to abandonment, however unconsciously it is playing out in the depths of their unconscious. As they are abandoned by certainty, so they grow desperate to reconstitute certainty's presumptive authority, its presumptive presence.

So, we begin to get a picture of why it is so difficult to get unstuck. The stuckness is not about what it is about, and what we are able to see is usually only a surface manifestation of what we don't see. What we don't see is the way in which this sensitive organism we are mobilizes its defenses, its projections, and its fixations on objects, behaviors, images, practices, codes, institutions, and dogmas precisely because they seem to offer some relief from the archaic anxiety to which we all are subjected.

None of us is free of addictive patterns—by this I mean *reflexive anxiety management systems*. Frankly, we have to have these systems, but they can come to manage us rather than the other way around. That is when the cost of the addiction accumulates. *Reflexive* means that our response is automatic, not reasoned, not nuanced nor differentiated, and replete with rationalizations assembled in advance to defend the behavior the moment it is questioned. Anxiety is ubiquitous and drives the human animal, so it is understandable why we would develop our protective techniques. Through repetition, these protections get locked in and become systems that take on a life of their own, becoming the titular governors of our separate kingdoms. It is typically these management systems that we vow to replace or transcend, but this also explains why they are so resistant to our wills. To replace the systems will mean we either replace them with other systems, perhaps even more pervasive and costly, or stand nakedly before our two greatest threats, overwhelmment and abandonment.

Accordingly, we either have to make peace with our stuckness and move on as best we can or risk the activation of the archaic anxiety that pools in the historic basement for all of us. If we can discern what the stuck place is really about, then we will have flushed a specific fear out of the morass of disabling anxiety. In most cases, that fear will not happen, but it could, and we carry always the memory of when it did happen and was too much for us. Such fears include implicit premises, such as "If I move forward on this front, I will be out there alone, or I will lose the understanding and support of loved ones or my tribe—and I will not be able to bear that."

Naturally, we do not think this consciously, for if we did, we might first realize that such will not happen, or second, that were it to happen, we could manage the cost, given that a resilient person has grown in place of the dependent, powerless child. But third, sometimes we have to go there, the place of the fear, in order to grow up, to recover our lives from all the assembled defenses, of which denial, repetition, and rationalization are the accomplices. Only in those moments when we take life on, when we move through the archaic field of anxiety, when we drive through the blockage, do we get a larger life and get unstuck. Ironically, we will then have to face a new anxiety, the anxiety of stepping into a life larger than has been comfortable for us in the past. This growth itself can be so intimidating that we often choose to stay with the old stuckness. We have to want something larger, really want it. We have to risk feeling worse before feeling better, and we have to risk the loss of the oh-so-comforting misery of stuckness.

# Chapter 8

# Come Back to Your Task

Plato argued that we are born "knowing," but the abrasions of daily life wear it away. We have all heard the story of the three-year-old confronting her newborn sibling, saying, "Tell me what it was like; I am forgetting already." The memory of the cloudless, umbilical Eden is already fading in the mind's eye. Once, reading an ancient Chinese text, I came across the image of "the man who lives in the House of Self-Collection." The image hit me with the shock of recognition, for I so often think on the corrosive costs of daily life, the multiple claims upon us, and the commitments legitimate and imposed, which only the metaphor of unraveling can summarize.

Jung observed that in virtually every case he attended, the person knew from the beginning what his or her task was. The presenting neurosis, the blockage, the obstacles that obscure the task are only the surface distractions from the implicit intimidation of really knowing what is right for us. But something within always does know what is right for us and what is wrong. We know as children, and what we know then gets overruled by the powers and principalities of the world and the need to fit in somehow.

Further, Jung pointed out that even our neuroses, our twists, turns, and permutations of soul, are efforts to heal something felt amiss. But in these reflexively arranged defenses against our hurts, we set up other consequences, other collateral damage. Anesthetizing oneself to the world is understandable, avoidance is strategic, and complicity is comforting, but each sets in motion an inauthentic response to the challenges of life. If we arrive at these places of momentary respite, something nags from within still, for adaptation is not resolution and flight from discord is not meaning. Jung nailed it: "A psychoneurosis must be understood, ultimately, as the suffering of a soul which has not yet discovered its meaning."[1] Notice that he does not rule out suffering, for suffering, as the medieval adage had it, "is the fastest horse to completion."

Often the flight from suffering leads to a trivialized life, a distracted life, an anesthetized life. The clear implication of Jung's position is that working one's way through to meaning—that is, to an enlarged view of one's dilemma and perhaps an enlarged view of one's own summons—can lead one through the valley of the shadow. He adds, "Among my patients, from many countries, all of them educated persons, there is a considerable number who came to see me not because they were suffering from a neurosis but because they could find no meaning in their lives or were torturing themselves with questions which neither our philosophy nor our religion could answer."[2]

I cannot count the times someone has said in the midst of analysis or a workshop, "I know I should . . . (fill in the blank)." How is it we can know and not carry through? This dilemma goes back to the chapter on stuckness for sure, and we need to remember that in those blockages, we are succumbing to an archaic anxiety of some sort: we fear we will be ridiculed, left alone, fall on our face, and so on. We all have those fears, yet deep within is that call again, that summons. How many talents have been neglected, opportunities aborted, risks rationalized away? Each one of those moments of postponement, rationalization, and deflection was when we turned our back on our own soul.

What, then, is our task? Two things: individuation and overcoming the specific obstacles the fates have placed on our path.

First, individuation—what is meant by that term? Too often the word seems to offer license to narcissism and, at best, seems a pathway to selfish self-interest over the needs of others. What Jung meant by the term is quite contradictory to these presumptions. Individuation is a religious summons, the flight from which leads to pathologies of all sorts—distorted relationships, anesthetizing or distracting behaviors that lead to a narrowing path, or a chronic dis-ease, the cure to which is never found in medications, new relationships, or new pursuits. As long as one is running from one's own soul, no achievement, no compromise, no accommodation will satisfy. Individuation is in fact *service*, but service to what?

When I was writing my book *What Matters Most*, the first thing that came to my mind, apart from the conventional answers of family, friends, and good work, was that one's life not be governed by fear. Fear is unavoidable, but a life in which fear calls the shots is one that results in terrible malformations of the soul. As we know, nature always demands its due, and so the soul, which is our metaphor for the fact that we are that meaning-seeking and meaning-creating animal, demands respect. I cannot tell you how many good folks have told me that they never wanted to be in their particular profession, but it pleased the parents, made them feel legitimate, or offered financial security. An equal number have said as much regarding their relational commitments, including, "The invitations were already sent out," "We had sunk too much money in the event to back out," and so on. Looking back on our lives, we may recognize many critical choices were driven by fears—fear of disappointing others, fear of embarrassment, fear of loss of family consensus, and so on. And often such fears made decisions for us, often to be unraveled over years of conflict, depression, anger, and further dithering.

Sooner or later our psyche weighs in with its reports because something inside is hurting, and the usual efforts to remove the hurt have failed. Naturally, a person would like to believe that the therapist possesses magic, or at least a multistep plan for the resolution of the hurt. Actually, therapists have only one plan, with many variations of course—namely, the challenge to live with the reality of one's own soul. How many times have I asked, "What do you think has produced this discord within you? Do you think your psyche is trying to tell you something by withdrawing its approval and support of where ego consciousness invests its energies?" These provocative questions are rhetorical tools to turn a person back on his or her own resources.

To step out into our lives, to come back to the task of becoming who we really are when not defined by roles, categories, or the expectations of others, is a most daunting summons. To counter the fear of stepping into the world as ourselves, I have often invoked that old chestnut: "How will you feel if conscious on your deathbed that you had not been here as yourself?" No one yet has suggested that they would feel okay about that dismal prospect. That tells me that something within each of us knows what is right for us and knows when we are living in *mauvaise foi*, or bad faith. Our soul can manage a great deal: suffering, loss, isolation, and much more if it feels that there is purpose to the suffering. It cannot long tolerate suffering without meaning nor abide our compromises with ourselves. As Jung pointed out, the smallest of things with meaning is infinitely greater than things without meaning. And meaning is defined by our souls, not our culture.

Coming back to our task also means that we have to show up as we are, adding our small but critically important piece to the mysterious puzzle of life. And we have to do it in the face of whatever obstacles the fates, the whimsical gods, or pernicious people in our histories have brought us. In other words, the meaning of our life will be a direct function of the degree to which we became more nearly ourselves, showed up as best we could in the face of the difficulties that life presented.

There is often a perverse satisfaction in self-sabotage, of slipping into our life-denying self-images, of turning away when the invitation is large, psychologically speaking. In those moments, we are asked to return to our task, the task of being who we are. So simple, so difficult, so profound. And that is our gift to the world, not as self-aggrandizement, not as self-inflation, but as the simple service to the soul. What can be more important in our journey, more intimidating, and more compelling than honoring the soul in this humbling way? While fate is often harsh and delimiting, most of us lack this excuse. We forget our task, our responsibility to our talents, to our interests, and to our unique perspectives on the world because it is easier to do so. We forget, simply forget. Yet something in us remembers and protests. So we dismiss the protests, the troubling dream, the fear that awakens us at three in the morning. We run from ourselves to places of security, of comfort, to the fantasy of fitting in.

I do not judge such a person, for I am one on many days, yet other days I face the fears, the lack of permission, and the intimidating largeness of it all, and show up as best I can. I cannot now say that I do not know, that I am ignorant or uninformed, nor can you anymore. We have made enough excuses in our lives, offered enough rationalizations, and evinced enough evasions, but something inside persists, shows up, troubles sleep, and asks more of us—and sooner or later we all have an appointment with our soul. Whether we show up, remember the divine task, remains to be seen.

# Chapter 9

# Choose the Path of Enlargement

A very effective instrument when in the face of blockages and difficult choices is to ask the very pragmatic question: "Does this choice enlarge me or diminish me?" I submit that usually we know the answer to that question immediately. If we don't know the answer, then it is important to continue the question, for its resolution will always appear: as a dream image, a sudden recognition in the middle of the night, an insight that occurs in the middle of traffic when the ego is not maintaining its usual vigilance against disturbing thoughts. And then we know the answer to that question. We should choose the path of enlargement, not service to wealth, power, fame, or the accolades of others, because it is what is asked of us by the soul. When we choose the small, we don't have to step into the large, which is quite comforting until we realize we are living small, diminished lives.

To be sure there are many forces in this world that contribute to diminishment. They are well known: poverty, lack of education, prejudice, dealing with a tilted playing field. But the biggest diminishment of all is the deep lesson derived from having been small, dependent, unknowing, and those matrices, repeated through our most formative years, feed diminishment, psychospiritual impoverishment, shame, and unworthiness.

Recall the common message of childhood: *The world is big, and you are not. The world is powerful, and you are not.* This message, over-learned, abides with us throughout all our journeys. What makes us timorous is the activation of the old paradigm with which we all grow up, that we are small and the world large. That message is corrosive to our sense of worth, our entitlement to possibilities, our right to dream. I am not endorsing grandiosity, inflation, hubris, or any other delusional denial of reality; however, most of us, quite simply, live lives too small for us.

In his various essays on personhood, Jung writes that the summons to personhood is a calling, a true *vocatus*, in the original sense of a calling from the sacred. To obey this calling is tantamount to religious obedience to that which is larger than we. And therein lies both the path and the conundrum.

We all know people who have excess entitlement, whose narcissistic inflation seems limitless, who do not respect the democracy of the grave. We also know people whose core insecurities have resulted in compensatory inflation. They are the power brokers of the world. They lie to the world because they have to lie to themselves. As the great American philosopher Pearl Bailey reportedly said, "Them's what's thinks they is, ain't." Their compensatory inflation is not what I am talking about. The attainment of personhood is not self-aggrandizement; it is answering a summons to step into oneself, to honor one's interests, talents, and callings, whether recognized by others or not.

In walking through the Smithsonian Museum of American Art, I am always moved by a work of sculpture there. Titled *The Throne of the Third Heaven of the Nations' Millennium General Assembly*, it is the life work of a gentleman who was a janitor for the federal government. By day, James Hampton swept the floors and cleaned the toilets. By night, he walked with gods and the vision they had vouchsafed him. Slowly, with tinfoil from a thousand pieces of chewing gum and the fragments discarded by a bored public passing through the buildings in his custodial care, he assembled his grand vision. I know no other artist with a vision this grand—including Michelangelo, who at least had patrons with deep pockets. Slowly, privately, he worshipped at the shrine of his particular genius.[1] This is a man I admire greatly. He did his work, honored his vision at home, in his garage, unseen by any until his death. He dialogued not with public support, or fame, or companionship, but with the really large.

We all have a calling. For some it will be found in our capacity for caring for the needs of the suffering world around us. For others it will be the work of hands. For some it will be the work of the mind that opens doors and shatters shackles. For still others it will be the exploration of the natural world. For some it will be pushing back the boundaries of our limited sense of the possible. But for all of us, there is a large summons.

From childhood on, we all felt that others had it together and we did not, that others knew what they were doing, while we clearly did not. But we have never been admitted into their doubts, their failings, their moments of moral cowardice, their shames. Only when we risk our own journey can we begin to pull back the projections we have on others. *Everyone* we meet is beset with their own problems. Most of the time they don't want you to know that, and they are also trying to figure out ways not to know that for themselves.

Because we learn early that the safe response often lies in our denial of the reality of our own feelings, we soon align against our personal authority, becoming strangers to ourselves. Because we grow facile in this self-denial, we forget over time that what we really feel matters. As a counterpoise, we must recall that we do not choose feelings. Feelings are autonomous responses of the organism to how things are going from its perspective. We can choose to ignore feelings, project them onto others, anesthetize them, and so on, but we do not choose them. It took me quite a while, as a thinking type, to realize this elemental truth. Having lived in an atmosphere where my feelings could so easily be discounted and realizing also that the expression of my feelings might further destabilize a tense environment, I soon became insulated against them. One turning point occurred in my early days as a college professor, when a student, no doubt meaning well, said, "I want to be just like you." "How so?" I asked. "To have no feelings," he said. I think he meant "cool" or something like that, and while I could not believe that his assessment was accurate, still his perception of me had to be based on something. It was, of course, one of many cracks in a policy of self-containment that had proved protective, but whose buffers had constituted a pathologizing gulf between persona and inner reality.

The memory of intimidation by the large constrains us all. To ask the question at critical junctures in our lives, of relationships, of careers, of lifestyles, may prove of decisive significance: Does this make me large, or does it make me smaller? We all remember moments in our lives when the choice was for the smaller, often safer, route, and the fact that we remember, that something in us aches, is itself a clue that the summons continues. No history of deflected choice, no life of shame, no patterns of self-defeating choices can be used as an excuse to remain small, psychologically speaking. Once we know, once we remember, we cannot not know.

To reiterate, the choice of the large is not in service to grandiosity or to inflation; it is quite the contrary. It is in service to our growing recognition that something else besides security, fitting in, and protection asks our recognition. Rather than be enslaved by our fears, in service to our limiting heritage or our debilitated, even devastated, history, we understand finally that we are called to something large. Our attitude toward others then changes. We grow less fearful, less suspicious, less needy, because we know that we have a calling to something else. It is natural to have fears of the world. Only a psychotic person would not. But it is a violation of our souls if we live our lives governed by our fears.

Ultimately, to step into the larger, we have to go *through* our fears. I have to emphasize go *through*. There is no magic, no set of five steps to dissolve the obstacles, no pill, no narcotic to make it all possible. There is only the going through and then realizing that we are on the other side of that issue. While the child is dominated, even devastated, by the loss of the approval of others, the person who goes through finds something within that supports, approves, and carries.

Friedrich Nietzsche had a peculiar aphorism that he expressed through his character Zarathustra. We are, he observed, a going under and a going through. We are an abyss, and we are the tightrope across the abyss. What are we to make of those conundrums? It is my belief that we go under by dying unto our old fears and old beliefs, and we go through by living our lives as best we can manage. I also suspect that by "abyss," Nietzsche underlined the magnitude of being. Nearly a century later, Martin Heidegger observed that the abyss was an "openness of being," rather than that which swallows us. When we remain prisoners to our complexes, and their history-bound, unimaginative purview, what else can we do but repeat our fugitive history? When we summon the timorous ego to the magnitude of our soul's intent, we step across something deep within ourselves that abides in the midst of the abyss—the most difficult going through. All those whom we admire in history had to go through something, and when they did, they learned on the other side that they were still there, though the world was different. Then they began to step into their possibilities and felt more completely the support of energies within.

In all of these years, I have met only one person who had this sense of the large within her even as a child, and the courage to live it. She called this inner voice, this guiding genie, TWIHAT: an acronym for That Which I Have Always Thought. For reasons I do not know, this stalwart sojourner sustained a trust in that voice we all have within us. She trusted it, lived it, went through hard times with it, and came out the other side, as we all will if we risk trusting our own individuation process, our own guiding spirit, and our invitation to choose the large over the small. Then we serve not our egos, but our world, and bring a greater contribution to it.

# Chapter 10

# What Gift Have You Been Withholding from the World?

I have never forgotten the observation of a sixty-five-year-old woman who began her therapy some decades ago by saying, "I cannot use the word *myself* without flinching." She went on to explain that she had been educated in a strict religious setting, and any child using the word *self* received admonition and corporal punishment. How those adults thought this helped children grow up into healthy adults is beyond me. Yes, they ensured that their charges would not become narcissists, but they also ensured that the children in their care would grow up fearful, neurotic, and diminished. And the same is true for most sports coaches I have observed. Most youth need a supportive, affirmative parent, someone who believes in them, not another derogating adult who tears down their fragile efforts.

There is no one I know who is without wounds to self-esteem. These wounds sometimes devastate people and govern their entire lives. They may have identified with the poverty around them, internalized the abuse they suffered or witnessed, and thereby collude with their victimization. Others find their resolve stoked, their desire to achieve triggered. Jung observed that usually behind the wound lies the genius of the person. That is to say, where we are hurt often quickens consciousness and resolve and abundant energy to persist, even prevail. The key is not what happens to us but how it is internalized and whether those messages expand or diminish our resilience. Again, the question is not what happened but what it makes us do or keeps us from doing. This is why two people can experience comparable life difficulties and move on in quite disparate ways.

We all wish to be seen, and many, perhaps most of us, are not. The rise of the Facebook era and selfie craze, the many blogs, all point to a desperate need to feel valued, seen, and hopefully affirmed. As Andy Warhol observed several decades ago, in America, sooner or later, everyone is famous for about fifteen minutes. The selfie preoccupation is all about being seen in some context—a celebrity, a historic site. Many of those shots are compensations for not feeling inherent value. I have always believed that successful parenting is found not in the splendiferous achievements of the child, who may only be compensating for the unlived life of the parent, but in the child who understands that he or she is seen and valued for who they are, not what they are supposed to do, achieve, become. It sounds so simple yet proves so rare.

Whether we believe that a purposeful God or random processes govern the universe is virtually irrelevant. What matters is to what degree we can accept ourselves as ourselves, with whatever shortcomings are common to this human estate. How often I have said, in discussing a compelling dream or some symptomatic resurgence, "Where do you think this came from inside of you?" and "What does it mean that something inside of you has expressed itself this way?" How often I have observed, "Do you now see that something inside of you exists independent of your will, your conscious life? Do you not see that something inside of you sees you and asks something of you?" Even the most troubling dream is an autonomous manifestation of something large within us that asks our respect, our dialogue.

Each of us has a gift, the essential gift of being who we are, with all the flaws, shortcomings, mistakes, and fears of which we are all so aware. One of the most pernicious influences of most religions, and a lot of unconscious parents, is the shaming process, the inevitable admonition to be perfect, to measure up to some abstract codes. As none of us is able to live a model of perfection, we wind up swimming in shame, overcompensating or self-sabotaging. When the woman shuddered in using the word *myself*, she was after all only serving the message that her distorted elders had imparted to her.

In the end, we are not here to fit in, to be well adjusted, acceptable to all, or to make our parents proud of us. We are here to be ourselves. Often that is not pretty, but it is honest. And our gift to the great mosaic of the world is our uniqueness. Each of us has something to bring to the mosaic of time that is unfolding in and through us whether we are aware or not. Some will possess a particular talent or capacity that is meant to be shared. I find myself never envying others or wanting to be someone other than myself. Knowing how flawed I am and how many mistakes I have made in life, I still feel that who and what I am is my humble gift to others. If there is an exception to my lack of envy, it would be only to those capable of making music, for music seems to me to be wholly transcendent and a symbolic gift to the universe.

When we think of the gift of ourselves, we usually revert to what is accepted, what is exceptional, or what might win approval. The flip side of this impulse may be seen in the desperate acts of the disenfranchised to become something notable through assassinations, acts of terror, or other egregious behaviors. For every thousand selfies, there is one Lee Harvey Oswald or Gavrilo Princip who makes his mark on history. Each act is the same: *I wish to be seen, to be valued, to be someone.* And as understandable as this desire surely is, how delusive the goal, how precarious the purchase on fame, importance, celebrity. Rather, our gift will best be found in the humble abode in which we live every day. Who I am, who you are, is the gift. No pretensions, no magnification necessary. They are merely compensations for self-doubt in any case.

The humble, brilliant Jesuit priest and poet Gerard Manley Hopkins saw it in the nineteenth century. In his poem "As Kingfishers Catch Fire," he describes,

> Each mortal thing does one thing and the same:
> Deals out that being indoors each one dwells;
> Selves—goes itself; *myself* it speaks and spells,
> Crying *What I do is me: for that I came.*

With his poetic sensibility, his metaphoric leap, he understands that the Self is not an object, not a noun, but rather a verb. The Self is always "selving," seeking expression. Even as the bulb "selves" into the flower, the organic center in each of us unfolds itself through us, whether conscious or not, assisted or impeded. Our selfhood is indwelling and forever incarnating in the world. To cry out, "What I do is me: for that I came," is not the desperate act of someone over-compensating; it is quite the contrary—it is humbling.

Some people's lives express themselves externally through the gifts of intellect, talent, or achievement of some sort or another. The world of selfies, the Guinness World Records, and the need for the fifteen minutes of fame are all compensations for not feeling one's inherent value in the first place. For most of us, however, the gift we may bring this world is found in moments of spontaneity where we add our small piece to the collective. It may be found in very private moments of reflection where we restrain our narcissistic impulses. It may be found in moments of compassion for others who struggle and falter in the face of their acquired, debilitating messages.

In recently witnessing Pope Francis, I was touched by his frequent pauses in the pageantry to affirm a child, a crippled person, a discarded soul, a prisoner in a concrete maze—all of them of value, all of them forgotten, left behind, but not forgotten in the eyes of this good man. His reminder touched many of us who do not espouse the specifics of his faith because he reminds us of the genuine gift that each being brings to this troubled world. It is not sentimentality to affirm the disaffirmed. It is a remembrance of the essential dignity of all being, and how in its various ways, it brings to the great puzzle a special piece never before seen in human history.

How many times people have said to me, "I have always wanted to . . ." (fill in the blank)—to write a book, learn to play the piano, fly a plane, and so on—yet all of those sentences also include a "but" that transitions the thought down the familiar old alley of flight, denial, repression, and disregard. The "but" covers a multitude of rationales, fears, and old messages that keep us from our essential selfhood, from our ordinary being that is our gift to the world. In asking what gift we are withholding, rather than some spectacular achievement, we are rather humbled to come before the reality of who we are and to realize that that is our most precious gift.

To be eccentric, not to fit in, to hear our own drummer, these are the signs of our bringing our gift, our personhood, to the table of life. It sounds so simple, but it is so difficult, not only because of all the disabling messages of the past but also because to be that gift asks us to let go and trust that something within us is good enough, wise enough, strong enough to belong in this world. How dare one disregard what is seeking expression through us, to cower in the darkness of fear, to resist the gift that illumines this otherwise colorless world.

# Chapter 11

# See the Old Self-Destructive Patterns

D on't you have to ask from time to time, "Why does my life keep working out this way?" or "Why are my relationships always ending?" or "Why don't I feel good about my life when I am trying so hard?" If a person hasn't asked these or similar questions, then he or she remains blissfully unconscious and may deserve what keeps happening. Jung once observed the only unforgivable sin is to choose to remain unconscious.

When we finally admit the obvious to ourselves, namely, that we are the only consistent player in that long-running soap opera we call our life, we begin to become conscious and possibly accountable. One of the best ways to get a sense of what is happening to us, through us, what is occurring in the unconscious, is to identify our patterns. We don't rise every day expecting that we will do the same dumb things, the same self-destructive things we have been doing for a long time, but chances are if we are still conscious at all at the end of the day, we will have done precisely that, repeated our self-destructive patterns. *But why?*

Recall from our earlier discussions that from infancy to the present moment, we "read" the world around us for messages about the world and about ourselves. This phenomenological reading is, of course, contingent on so many variables: the varieties of the world presented to us, our specific cultural and personal contexts, the models around us, and elements unique to our genetics, character, and disposition. Thus, the identical external event can be internalized quite differently, messaged differently, from person to person. But those readings become our maps of the world, our marching orders, our understandings of self and world, even our contracts with the world. They are, of course, highly variable, ideocentric, prejudicial. They serve as the lenses through which we see the world, interpret it, and get our instructions. Thus, we become servants to, even prisoners of, our maps, our instructions, our marching orders.

For one person the core instruction seems to say: "Hide out; don't be seen. You don't matter. Don't expose yourself to risk." That core message, repeated daily, leads to a fugitive life, a life of diminished possibilities and continuous disappointments. For another person, the core message seems to be: "Step in; assume responsibility. You are charged with fixing the other, putting out the fire." Such a person often later sees his or her life has been in service to the troubles, the pathologies, unfinished business of others, rather than to his or her own life. For still another, the core message is translated as: "Become a star; be outstanding. You have to make up for the unhappy life of your father or your mother. Your life doesn't matter. What matters is how you rescue them from sadness, from loss, from bitterness."

The organism that we are is quite conservative in its operations. It prefers predictability to the unplanned, the known over the unknown, and the familiar over the foreign. Sometimes something bursts inside of us, wanting to live, wanting to become in the world, even as it is opposed by other agencies that overrule, veto, and distract, until the impulse passes, the desire is drained. Clinging to the present, with all its predictable ends, is very seductive. One of the reasons for this self-sabotage arises from free-floating anxieties that whisper in our ear such sweet nothings as: "You are not up for this. What makes you think you can do that? It will lead to isolation and loss of the love and understanding of others. You will be all alone. You will fail, be ridiculous." We all know those voices. If we don't hear them consciously, we may be sure that they are still being whispered to us through the unconscious.

I recall a client who was going through a very difficult dark night of the soul. He had lived a very productive life, when judged by the expectations of his tribe. He had been faithful to the values of his family and religious training, yet he was pulled underground by a near-suicidal depression. If he had done all the right things, if he did what he was supposed to, why did he suffer this Job-like hour, this grievous appointment with darkness? In the middle of this night-sea journey, he had a dream in which he was descending into the depths of a body of water. He could breathe underwater and be conscious of the descent. Images of his history flashed by him. He then saw at the bottom of the sea a skull image that said, "And then came the great turning away." And then he awoke and puzzled over this strange, vatic message. What turning away? What was the meaning of all that?

As we wrestled with this dream, what came to him was an early vocational calling, but at a key moment in his early years, he suddenly shifted his career and chose a safer path. Looking back on that turn in his life, he asked himself why he had made that choice, and the only answer that made any sense was that he was responding to fear when he demurred, stepping away from his calling toward a more conventional channel. What fear? What was that about? In the end, the best we could make conscious was that the fear had to do with the need for acceptance, for consensual support, and the debilitating fear that he was not up to the challenge that his vocation would have demanded of him. And so, without "choosing," he chose, as we all tend to choose on any given day. He chose the safer path, the lesser journey, until finally his psyche registered its autonomous dismay and weighed in with its perspective. In doing "the right thing," he had done the wrong thing, and so do we all on many occasions. We choose the strongly ingrained, we follow the paradigms, and we stick to the known, even when the known leads only to ennui, boredom, depression, anesthetizing treatments, or chronic divertissement.

Without the autonomy of the unconscious, the larger part of our being, without its registrations, evaluations, and critiques, we would never know what was right for us. Hardly anyone deliberately sets out on a false course, a life-denying aversion to the spirit's summons, yet many have done this, over and over.

Recently, a woman whom I have seen for two years acknowledged her chagrin. She still feels like a little girl, following the script expected of her, even as she has a position of high responsibility in a midsize corporation. Why does she still feel like a little girl, despite her significant responsibilities in the work world? Something inside her, and in many of us, still clings, still feels provisional. We presume if we follow our scripts, do the right thing, and do what we are supposed to do, we will be led to a place of well-being. We believe we will experience reward, satisfaction, and truly be a big person, as we presume so many others to be. Being a big person, however, means more than walking around in a big body and playing big roles in life. In the face of such compelling, mostly unconscious, messages, we recall that most commonly we serve them, play them out, and they in turn create those pernicious patterns. Or we run from them, spend our lives seeking to compensate—"anything but like my mother" or "I won't repeat my father's life"—but we remain defined still by that "other" we wish not to be, an other that exercises an inordinate shaping influence in our lives. Or, thirdly, we seek to "fix" the problem, alter the tapes, employ anesthetizing anodynes of various kinds, live lives of distracting frenzy, or fix the problems in others (a common stratagem of those in the helping professions).

The first adulthood is still largely governed by the power of the messages, the models we observed and internalized, and the instructions we receive from family of origin, institutional religion, cultural contexts, and the like. Can we say such an adulthood, however sincere, however "successful" in its fulfillment of these messages, is a real adulthood or the journey we are really supposed to live?

The second adulthood comes only when a person, for whatever reason, is called to accounts—a sinking marriage, an affective storm, a moment of terrifying emptiness at three in the morning. Yet this hammer blow begins the possibility of a turn to a second, different kind of adulthood. A second adulthood is not a simple transformation into a different person, a metanoia from which the river flows in a quite different direction. The old order, the familiar scripts, hang on. They have enormous staying power, which is why simple behavioral changes and cognitive shifts are so seldom lasting. What one finds is that the perduring power of the old cannot be underestimated, for it is a de facto reflex whose purpose is protective, even if its outcome is constrictive. It takes an enormous amount of suffering, resolve, or life-changing circumstances for one to awaken sufficiently to take on these tyrannical powers of repetitive adaptation and service to anxiety management. If there is such a thing as the soul, then it is the soul that ultimately tips the balance toward change, toward a more authentic stance in the world. Jung observed that a neurosis is always found in the flight from authentic suffering. Naturally, no one wants to suffer, but Jung's observation suggests that there is a distinction between authentic and inauthentic suffering.

History is replete with examples of people like us who have gone through this death and rebirth process. I have experienced it and witnessed it in dozens upon dozens of analysands through the last four decades. There is no going forward without a death of some kind: a death of who we thought we were and were supposed to be; a death of a map of the world we thought worthy of our trust and investment; a death of expectations that by choosing rightly we could avoid suffering, experience the love and approval of those around us, and achieve a sense of peace, satisfaction, arrival home. But life has other plans it seems; indeed, our own souls have other plans. And there is a terrible price to pay for ignoring or fleeing those intimations and summons to depth.

Recognizing the self-destructive patterns in our lives, those places where we sabotage ourselves through avoidance, adaptation to the collective, or flight into the trivial, the conventional, the acceptable, is only the beginning. Those psychic reflexes, those complexes, will be with us the rest of our lives. So often I have heard people complain that their dreams keep coming up with the same motifs, the same images, and so I have had to respond, "Would you prefer someone else's dreams, someone else's problems?" Or people will berate themselves for not getting past a certain problem or feel that their work has been in vain when an old issue rears its ugly head in an unexpected way. These moments are inevitable. I called them "hauntings" in a recent book because we live in historic structures with spectral presences of all kinds, friendly ghosts, pernicious ghosts, the ghosts of other people, times, and places, with congested paths ahead of us.

Recognizing the patterns, especially the self-destructive patterns, is the first step. Then comes taking them on, for the rest of one's life. Taking them on requires risk, courage, perseverance, and showing up more days than not. Some days the possibility of a larger life wins; other days the ghosts win. One has to know that every day is a war between the constrictive colloquies of history and the invitation to the high seas of the soul. But such a venture is what our life is about, what real adulthood is about, and what the journey of the soul demands.

# Chapter 12

# What Is the Bigger Picture for You?

Our pictures of self and world are framed early, and as we have demonstrated, we seldom see a world larger than our frame allows. And yet, this is precisely why we have to come to recognize, respect, and dialogue with the other autonomous centers of intelligence within each of us that are wise in their ways and also invested in our well-being. This means the almighty ego has to realize that it is not really the master of the house, that there are many agencies that go bump in the night, many organs of special interest that play out their agendas, and equally that there are many healing mechanisms at work in the daily recalibrations of the organism as it seeks to survive and prevail in this world. Such mechanisms include dreams and symptoms—both autonomous, qualitative expressions of the psyche with which a genuine, respectful, and humble dialogue can lead to a much greater amplitude of vision, as well as a deeper, richer experience of the unfolding mystery of our own being.

When we consider "What is the bigger picture for me?" what comes up on the screen most often is: "Can I get the mortgage paid, the kids through school, find some partner to make my life whole, achieve a sense of satisfaction and well-being?" Where do we stand in relationship to the larger in our life, given that our complexes, our protective mechanisms, are driven by small concerns—important surely, but still small in the larger schemata of life.

When we reflect on the larger picture for our parents, what comes up? Do we find, for example, that our worries, concerns, preoccupations, and obsessive behaviors are the same and replicate their anxieties?

If so, did we not just acquire them by internalizing their examples? Do we find our parental models were naturally caught in the questions and values of their time, leaving aside for the moment whether we are equally caught in the questions and values of our time? For example, for most of our parents, the power and role of the collective was much more influential than in our time. For them, exclusion from collective expectations was a form of hell. So whatever our parents thought, longed for, and suffered, most of them carried on in daily silence. When there were aberrations, such as people of different faiths marrying, people of different races mingling, or people of alien values expressing themselves, there was a generalized reaction and always, always intimidating judgments.

More recently, a nationally known woman told our mutual friend that she would not attend a class or lecture at the Jung Center because one of her children had seen a Jungian analyst in couples therapy and . . . got a divorce! In other words, no consideration of what might be best for the soul of her adult child, let alone the child's right to their own decision even entering her purview. According to this woman, the role of the therapist was to keep the couple together, perhaps at all costs. I grieve, more than judge, the world of our parents, because for them their world was so circumscribed by socialized roles, categories, scripts, and expectations—and the sanctions for those who did not conform quite severe.

Similarly, their "big" religious picture was rather small as well, in my view. And even today, the mainstream religions have lost an enormous number of adherents—some split off by the enticements of the modern secular world, while others learned that there is a larger world out there, larger than the old tribal values—so that we are no longer constrained by the historic lens of our antecedents.

And yet, in the Western world at least, the only organized religions that grow and thrive are based on two diminishing perspectives. On the one hand are the fundamentalists, who respond to the changes of the modern and postmodern worlds by seeking to reconstitute the old values, the old normative ethics, and the old hierarchies of authority. Theirs is a community driven not by genuine experience, not by authentic conviction, but by anxiety and a "treatment plan" that reestablishes a known, albeit limited, world and its containing choices.

The other branch of institutional religion that grows is the one that has shaken hands with secularism, the gospel of prosperity, the motivating agenda of well-coifed, slick purveyors with polished programs, telling us that getting right with the Big Guy upstairs will lead to happiness, prosperity, and peace. Very seductive, those offerings, but they have the staying power of cotton candy, offering richness but leaving a gritty substance on the palate.

Which of these "bigger pictures" is worse: the one that infantilizes people by evoking omnipotent parent complexes in them, making them feel guilty, inadequate, and unworthy, or the one that offers an untroubled path but betrays them in the inevitable dark hours that come to all of us? Which is worse, that which infantilizes or that which trivializes? It is hard to decide between these two perversions.

For sure, we have good-faith efforts to address the role of anxiety in our journeys, with treatment plans ranging from Reinhold Niebuhr's Serenity Prayer, to sundry forms of Eastern meditation, to a panoply of narcotics and a vast pharmaceutical industry devoted to numbing our angst. Additionally, we have generated a popular culture whose twenty-four-hour buzz offers a life of distraction, divertissement, and various anodynes in seductive packaging. So what then is a big picture for any of us?

On the front we have traditionally called religion, I agree that we are religious creatures at heart, no matter what our preoccupations, addictions, distractions, or confessions. In his *Systematic Theology*, theologian Paul Tillich asserted that religion is where one expresses one's "ultimate concern." If one's ultimate concern is to gain material abundance, many millions so worship. We are surrounded by people who possess more than people have ever possessed before in history. And how are their lives faring? How are their souls? Recent studies indicate that the basic annual income in the United States necessary to achieve a state of relative well-being, even "happiness," is around $50,000.[1] At various stages above that figure, no appreciable increase in the sense of well-being is evident. In other words, a natural concern for providing food on the table, a roof over one's head, and clothing for one's person is quite understandable, but beyond that, more is not really more, or at least more is not enough to be more. What does that tell us?

There is something in all of us that longs for a bigger picture. Something in us wishes for connection, wishes to reframe the trivial in our daily lives, the pettiness with which most of our systems operate. If we look thoughtfully at the enterprise we call the great religions, with their rich anthologies of wisdom, their timeless stories, and their insights into the permutations of the human soul, we can still draw much that is useful in this wired world in which we swim. But we all have to uncover some other criteria by which we evaluate the instructions to which we are all in service most of the time. As we know, the complexes we serve, the autonomous clusters of history within us, have a historically generated, time-bound message for us. As long as they are operating, we are serving the small world they embody. Again, were there no psychopathology, no restlessness of the soul, why would we ever question these received, limited, fractal frames? And so, similarly, whatever our received religious values, I suggest some other criteria for evaluation.

First, does our encounter with the rich mystery of life repeatedly call upon us to reframe our understanding of self and world? If it does not, I submit that we are less linked to certainty than stuck in constriction, locked into an emotionally contained, imaginatively stunted partial view. Yes, we know that having to reframe our concepts, practices, understandings, and even values generates anxiety, but a mature spiritual position will oblige us to tolerate more anxiety than we wish. An authentic journey will ask us to embrace contradictions, suffer ambiguity, and not fall into either-or thinking, which is so characteristic of the immature or the frightened mind.

A mature spirituality will be one in which we encounter more mystery than is comfortable. After all, the things we can understand, tolerate, fixate in concepts are surely not the mystery. The mystery will always transcend our desires for clarity and certainty. But how much of that can we tolerate? F. Scott Fitzgerald has a character in one of his short stories who defines the first-rate mind as one that can hold opposites in tension without having to fall on one side of the ledger or the other. And Jung added that ordinary ideas are easily contradicted by other ideas, but for profoundly truthful ideas, their opposites are also true. Therefore, only paradox can begin to approach the magnitude of the universe in which we float.

*A mature spirituality does not offer certainty; it offers mystery.* It offers depth, it obliges reframing our understandings, and it requires growing up psychospiritually.

Considering the larger picture for each of us on a very personal level requires that we reflect on Jung's concept of individuation. By *individuation*, he does not mean narcissism, ego aggrandizement, or being measured by any external achievements. Individuation means submission, not ego triumph or transcendence of the ordinary. It means surrendering the life we wanted or expected, for that which the gods or the soul (whatever metaphor you prefer) calls for. Most of the people we admire in the history of this planet are people who did not have easy, comfortable lives; in fact, most of them suffered horribly. But we admire them because they won their way through to incarnate their unique gifts in this world. Their gift sometimes took the form of prophetic utterances, scientific discoveries, social visions, creative expressions, or acts of self-abnegating compassion. But most of all, they were the willing vehicles for Being that seeks expression though our individual beings.

The bigger picture for all of us is found in asking from time to time, "What is my life about, really?" We are all deeply invested in the details of daily life, and usefully so, but we are more than economic animals, more than social tokens on a large board, more than perpetually hungry animals. We are souls in the world of flesh, spirits in the world of perpetually decaying matter. What does it mean to be here? To what am I called? What values, traits, and capacities must I embody in my life? These are the kinds of questions that call us out of the trivial, that help us reframe our frustrations and disappointments and step into something larger than fitting in, being successful, being safe, and being accepted by everyone. These moments are far from comfortable, but they are energizing and lead us from one developmental stage to the next, and the one beyond that, stretching out into the emergent future.

Then we are alive, not just going through the motions. We are alive because we are serving life more than security, serving growth more than comforting stasis, serving the soul more than the anxious, distracted, and fugitive crowd.

# Chapter 13

# Choose Meaning over Happiness

Happiness seems such a wonderful place to visit, even better to abide in. The world is full of happy pills, happy places, happy promises. No sane mind would argue against happiness, surely. If we all could just be happy, everything would be fine. Wouldn't it? You won't find me inveighing against happiness. Indeed, it is even in the Declaration of Independence of the United States, and where could a happier place be than in such a nation? "Life, liberty, and the pursuit of happiness," it says, right there in black and white. Can't argue with that. While scholars suggest that the word *happiness* as used by Jefferson in that time and place and for that specific topic means the right to pursue the course of life one wishes, ours surely is still a culture devoted to the pursuit of happiness.

And what does that mean exactly? I am to be happy that I have a good job, food on the table, loving companions, and a roof over my head? I am grateful, for sure. But would then happiness require me to forget the many imperiled not very far from my door, those suffering from poverty, intractable pain, and no prospects for amelioration? Does it require that I forget the corruption spread round the world, from the highest councils to the lowliest villages? Does it allow me to forget all the injustices, unrequited murders, holocausts, pogroms, and natural disasters that are part of the lamentable catalogs of history? What does it take, what drug, what anodyne, what fantasy, to allow me to be happy in the face of what any thoughtful person knows? Am I to take those happy pills? Distract with the sundry divertissements of our time? Am I simply to finesse the question and believe in another life after this sordid mess that will redeem all this—restoring life to those slain, comfort to those in pain, and justice to those betrayed by their societies?

Or is it that I have failed to read the right self-help books, those that promise five easy steps will take me there or thirty days of this or that will lead me into the blessed place? Have I failed to apply those ready recommendations with insufficient alacrity, devotion, and rigor, or have I suffered a dilatory will, a slothful indolence, or perhaps I am to sup only from a sophomoric susurrus of cynicism?

Or is it possible that happiness is simply the latest in a pathetic parade of palliative panaceas to emanate from a culture that longs to be ahistorical, to forget what must be remembered, that is too busy with trivia to be bothered with all this stuff? Our religions have, by and large, lost the capacity to link people to depth, to mystery. Capitalism and communism are systems that in their quite similar ways are generated by people who game the system and privilege the few. No institution is not compromised by self-interest and psychopathology. So where does that leave us?

As a youth, I believed with all the naiveté and sincerity of youth that if I read enough, learned enough, and figured enough out, I would arrive at some sunlit plane where, free from conflicts and compromise, I would be in charge of my life and happy. While I have been blessed more than most souls on this planet and am daily mindful of that gift, I learned early that achieving one's goals always leaves one hungry for the next level. If one is good, two must be better, right? I told myself that my goal was never money or power, but a sense of completion, of sustained satisfaction. Little did I know then that such an achievement would itself be a form of hell, for all closed systems are engines of boredom, stultification, and spiritual death.

So today I submit to you that the happiness metric is a poor measure of a life. Happiness that is in any way based on denial, distraction, or ignorance is an affront to the soul and its depth. In my view, what abides is meaning. But what is *meaning*?

The ancient Greek philosopher Epicurus wrestled with this same question. Today, Epicurus is memorialized in "epicurean," which typically translates to "fine dining." Well, fine dining can be delightful, sometimes even memorable, but once the experience is complete, its effect passes. Having finished a full, luxurious meal, no one wants to begin another one, and another one after that (Rome's ancient vomitoria notwithstanding). So, Epicurus reasoned, given that we are rather overtly pleasure-seeking, pain-avoiding creatures, what might provide us with some sustained pleasure? It was not eating, for even the pleasures of the palate provide only transient satisfaction; once satisfied, the same object of desire becomes repulsive. So, what then abides, if not fine dining?

The philosopher concluded that the most sustained pleasure available is not of the senses but philosophy itself. He may not be far off. While philosophy is not everyone's first choice for pleasure, one suspects Epicurus concluded that the state of one's mind is perhaps the key to this question. If philosophy provides continuing enterprise and continuing discovery, it might thereby bring continuing pleasure.

My spin on this issue is that the way we attain some sustained satisfaction is in fact linked to our attitudes. Surely, Gautama, who became the Buddha, one who "sees" through the delusions of desire, was on the same track. He suggested that to become "no-minded," to relinquish attachment to our desires, and to be wholly present to every moment is a far better way to attain satisfaction in the experience of this quite brief life journey. I certainly have acquired some corrective ideas from his thoughts, but I remain, for better or for worse, a creature of desire. Some of those desires are tangible and concrete and others quite abstract, but I do not forswear them. They are, finally, who I am. We are desire, Eros, and Eros is a god, the youngest because renewed daily in all movements of life, and the oldest because central to the fundaments of all life-forms. I also forswear any promises of an afterlife that offers to make all this mess acceptable. If there is an afterlife, then it is not this life, the one I inhabit, and if it exists, then it would so radically transform life as we know it that it remains incomprehensible. I really doubt that state exists, and I no longer long for it. What I do long for is an experience of this life that I would not trade for eternity in those elysian fields. And I can report that I have had such moments here on this sordid planet.

Those experiences here may better be described as meaningful rather than happy, though often such moments are happy while they last. More commonly, such moments are more moving engagements with others, with mystery, with curiosity and its discoveries, than anything the world names happiness. Indeed, some of these moments occur in the context of great suffering. I am moved when I see strangers, in moments of natural disaster perhaps, reach out to each other in compassion and support, forgetting for the while the issues that divide them. I am moved when I see the resilience of the human spirit in people who have been battered by life. To see them survive, move through suffering, and reach a different place makes me happy, for the while, because it floods me with meaning. To work with people in their traumas, disappointments, even despair, is so meaningful I cannot describe it. To be allowed on a daily basis to share the journey with such souls is so meaningful that I am humbled by the magnitude of the privilege. To be able to share with others what little I have learned is profoundly meaningful.

If happiness is the goal, then everything becomes contextual. To the thirsty person, a glass of water is happiness, though a flood is disaster. To the frightened person, the moment of rescue is happy, until the next peril emerges. And so on. Happiness is transient, but meaning abides.

But what is meaning, or what is the meaning of meaning?

Is not meaning so contextual, so idiosyncratic that every person, every hour will provide a new definition? Absolutely. Meaning is individual and contextual. As we all know, two people can have the same encounter, and one is bored or frightened, while the other is exalted, moved to tears. We cannot say to anyone else that this painting is meaningful, this music worth your devotion, this concept worth your life. And why not? Because meaning is an organ of the soul. The decisive arbiter is the soul, the psychological reality in which our lives unfold.

What we find, if we pay attention to the expressions of the psyche—our symptoms, our sudden insights, our compensatory dreams, our insurgent feeling states—is that our souls are constantly registering an opinion. This opinion is very little like public opinion, for it is the vote of one against the many. Such an opinion may make us uncomfortable, isolate us, or send us on a journey we fear, but it is the voice within that expresses the enduring opinion of the soul. To ignore this expression, which we all learn to do early on, means that we become strangers to ourselves. But the repressed returns in moments of sudden impulse, uncontrolled outbursts, troubling dreams, and most of all, in the erosion of meaning from our lives.

The more we give ourselves to the security of the known path, the more acceptable we may feel, but something in us does not accept this bad-faith arrangement. The more we are part of comforting consensus, the less we feel ourselves. The more we find approval from without, the more the psyche has to withdraw approval, until we feel drained, burned out, and depressed. In the unconscious pursuit of happiness, the soul finds aridity, one-sidedness, and a narrowing of focus. In the experience of meaning, we are asked to trust something deep within. We all know that. We all knew that as children, but given our powerlessness and lack of overt alternatives, we all learned to brush aside these internal promptings.

What excuse, then, do we have today? We are not powerless. We have learned an amazing amount about the world, about ourselves, about what works for us and what doesn't, what abides and what is ephemeral. What excuse then, today? Have we not all learned that the violation of that which lies so deeply within us, this inner voice, this inner certainty, this inner support, keeps showing up, despite our disdain, collusion, cowardice, and flights from the large?

We may be sure of one thing: the soul never leaves us. Whatever that inner essence is, it abides, it persists, and it keeps showing up. It knows the difference between a contextual happiness and an abiding meaning. It knows and persists in reporting to us in ways that befuddle our conscious ploys, rationalizations, and evasions. Remembering what knows us better than we know ourselves, we find ourselves less distracted by the seductions of happiness. In those moments of re-cognition of what we have always known, we more likely undertake paths confirmed by that deep place as meaningful. And as we experience such meaningful engagements, sacrifices, difficult passages, and challenges along the way, we are flooded from time to time, but only for a time, with happiness.

# Chapter 14

# Honor, Finally, What You Left Behind, and Seize Permission to Be Who You Are

Rousseau began his powerful *Confessions* with the sentence, "Man is born free, and everywhere is in chains." We might add a sentence to that: "We are born whole, and everywhere are fractured." To each statement one must ask the essential question Why? For Rousseau, the why is answered in his analysis of social institutions, how great ideas become institutionalized and impersonal and perpetuate themselves at the cost of their founding principles. So too must we consider the idea of wholeness an elusive goal; however, we also have to ask why it is we are so much at odds with ourselves, why it is that we are so often haunted by the unlived life, so often soured by the "shoulda-coulda-wouldas" of life.

We also know that we cannot stuff everything into this life. Every time we choose one thing, we exclude a dozen others. If we could live a serial existence, we might have a dozen opportunities to follow a talent, an interest, a curiosity, but we don't. Given the extended life most moderns are living, compared to that of our predecessors, we certainly have the opportunity for several different jobs, professions, friends, lifestyles, even emotional commitments. When we recall that in the classical era, the average length of life was the midtwenties, and only forty-seven in 1900 in North America, we realize how fortunate so many of us are to have the opportunity to change course, to pick up missing pieces, to go back to that we left behind.

So, what did we leave behind? For most of us, we left natural talents and enthusiasms behind for all sorts of reasons, including social conditions such as poverty, lack of education, and constricted opportunities. Many of us left behind joy, spontaneity, creativity, and enthusiasm, given the battering that so many acquire along this journey we call our life. For some, they are very specific talents, callings, curiosities, but the "permission" to pursue them seems abridged at best and missing at worst.

We cannot overemphasize the fact that many people live in emotionally, imaginatively constricted environments. When a neighbor child began music lessons, it was suggested to me as a youth that I not associate with him anymore because his mere access to music and the lessons required put him in an economic and social stratum beyond my family's. While this notion seems absurd at this remove, it was very real for my parents and therefore very real for me at that time. My father had been pulled from the eighth grade and sent to work in a factory when hard times came. My mother managed to graduate high school and work as a secretary. Both of them felt wholly defined by these economic and cultural limitations and meant no harm when they insisted that my brother and I be contained by them also. They discouraged our trying out for athletic teams and theatrical productions because they wanted to spare us disappointment and heartache. Similarly, joy and spontaneity were suspect because they threatened the predictable. And what was predictable? Hardship, disappointment, and disillusionment. Even worse, revealing emotions publicly made one vulnerable.

I was blessed by having both parents in my life, yet from each I learned to leave my feelings behind—spontaneity, anger, joy, and hope as well. Only in later years, when the psyche rebelled, did I begin to come back to these personal treasures left behind. While these last observations might seem judgmental, in fact, I spend a part of these days lamenting, not blaming, and having deep compassion for my parents' generation's struggles. There were no possibilities of therapy, no supportive world for them. Like so many of their generation, my parents took what came to them and did their best. Who could ask for more? I don't.

And yet, we all have to weigh the cost of history, examine its effects, and apply that telling question: What does that history make you do, or what does it keep you from doing?

These personal examples are factual, and they are far exceeded in the lives of children who had much, much worse, as I have seen personally in therapy. As we have noted, we all acquire enormous messages from our environmental settings—family dynamics, religion, education, social contexts, zeitgeist—and all provide compelling messages to serve, run from, or try to solve somehow. All of us internalize these fortuitous events, "message" them, and accumulate a provisional story about who we are and what we are supposed to do and not do. Accordingly, the greatest obstacle to a satisfying life remains the risky permission to live our lives as the soul desires.

Early on, all of us learned that permission was conditional. If one moved too much or not enough, in one direction or another, or expressed a deeply felt conviction, there were often sanctions, ranging from punishment to the withdrawal of approval. Either one of those retributive encounters can be devastating to a child. Just today I was speaking with a man in his eighties, a great success in his chosen career, yet he was speaking of how he seized up when he had to make certain kinds of decisions. When we examined the wiring in these decisions, it all came down to having grown up with a very narcissistic, insecure parent who severely punished deviations from strict compliance to her will. That he would be suffering the activation of these archaic anxieties decades later is not surprising, but it is not acceptable that his life still be run by the emotional needs of a woman dead these many decades.

But when we examine our own inhibitions, our hedging of bets, or our various compromises with the world, we also find such wiring reaching into our emotional basements. Sadly, that wiring will never go away, given its deep programming in the most vulnerable, impressionable stage of our formation. On the other hand, a natural growth process occurs in each of us, and sometimes we just outgrow these old fears, inhibitions, and constrictions. Other times it takes a depression or a series of disturbing dreams to get our attention and demand a larger life.

Through the years I have found no matter how accomplished the life, as measured by the often superficial parameters of popular culture, most people lack elemental permission to be who they are or to give voice to the magnitude of soul that exists within them. I am not talking at all about narcissistic self-indulgence. Rather, I am talking about the permission to let be what is within one's nature and allow it expression in forms that are not harmful to self or others.

In 1948, the Israeli Jungian scholar Erich Neumann published his pivotal work *Depth Psychology and the New Ethic*. Most of our history has been defined by normative ethics, prescriptive dos and don'ts. Adherents claim these desiderata are dictated by gods, some by the elders of the tribe, and others by venerated scriptures, traditions, and institutions. But nature always rebels and seeks its own expression. When we deny nature, it rebounds with compensatory dreams, symptoms, lapses, even somatic disorders. The "return of the repressed" as analysts call it.

But Neumann critiqued even the Freudian notion of sublimation, namely, finding a satisfactory form for the expression of the forbidden. This, he felt, was an evasion of the reality of the soul. The soul was not some unearthly, feathery thing, but our deepest essence, grounded in body and blood and desire. For Neumann the "new ethic" values consciousness over all things. One must become conscious of one's capacity for "evil," for the expression of those values contrary to our desire for ourselves, what Jung called the shadow. And one must honor them and sometimes suffer them, however contradictory they may seem to be. It is no small summons to have to deal with the pettiness that lies within us, the murderous rage, the pusillanimity, and cowardice, but what we refuse to face still spills into the world one way or another. The new ethic means one struggles to become as conscious as one can manage, and then one is accountable for all that one has made conscious, including our darker moments and motives.

Neumann was not, nor am I, calling on one to concretize the murderous impulses within, the lustful, cheating, petty parts of our personalities, nor the grandiose, inflated, narcissistic parts. Rather one is asked to pay attention and notice that they are, as the Latin playwright Terence noted two millennia ago, really part of who we are: "nothing human is alien to me."[1]

Once in a while one finds a person whose parents, or other formative influences, granted permission, but it is very rare and, of course, requires the fortuity of a supportive cultural setting as well. Permission is something that can be given if the parents not only affirm the child in his or her struggles, but also, even more importantly, live rich, full lives themselves. As Jung famously noted, no burden is greater for a child than the unlived life of the parent. What they have not faced in their lives remains a glass ceiling, a constriction that either the child serves or has to spend a lot of effort breaking through.

For most of us, however, for the great majority of the gifted, accomplished persons I have known, permission is not something given but something to be seized. One of the virtues of mortality, if one wishes to look for such a virtue, is the reminder that choices really do matter and that the issue of permission to make those choices is now critical and necessary. It may well lead one to realize that a life managed by fear is a life unlived. In the cases where I attended those overtly dying, most came to conclude that the interim provided them an urgent summons to a larger life. But does it take the imminence of departure to bring us to that urgency? I hope not. Many in the context of therapy discover that what has depressed them, what they sought to distract, or anesthetize, or flee, is actually the larger life that wishes expression through them. The moment we realize that our life is really in our own hands, that it is a spiritual summons to be honored, and that we deprive others by not bringing our more developed selves to share, then we realize permission is not something given—but something to be seized. And from that, a larger life, a life of service to a force greater than we are, begins. And from that turn, we get our life back, the life intended by the gods in the first place. As Jung observed once, life is a short pause between two great mysteries. I cannot imagine a better, more succinct definition of life than that—though I add that it is up to us to make that pause as luminous as possible.

# Chapter 15

# Exorcise the Ghosts of the Past That Bind You

W e all live in haunted houses and sleep in memory's unmade bed. What do those metaphors mean? Do you not wonder from time to time how your life is turning out, why the repetitions, why the patterns emerge—especially those that prove harmful to yourself or others? Just how free are we when we make critical decisions? No one rises in the morning and thinks, *Today I will do the same stupid things I have done for decades.* But chances are we will. And why?

Our ancestors believed in ghosts, the spirits of the dead, the existence of malevolent powers in the universe, and the possibility of captivation by those powers. Their beliefs arose from the fact that our psychological energies are reflexive in character, invisible to the mind's eye, even as their consequences in the world are visible. One of the ways to begin to reflect on these matters is to consider that we don't do stupid or counterproductive things intentionally, or rarely so; we do things that make sense to our emotional state at the time. We do what is logical given the emotional premises under which we operate in any given moment.

As we have seen, we all begin reading our environment—family of origin, popular culture, the zeitgeist—for clues as to what the world is about and how we are to comport ourselves to ensure safety and a modicum of satisfaction of our needs. Because acquired early, before rationality, before comparative experience, before our capacity to fend for ourselves, those premises lead us to evasive, controlling, or compliant behaviors. Those behaviors evolved early on in our formation and become an operational sense of self. Years later, these conditioned reflexes, these protective programs, are hardwired, constitute a shadow government of unchallengeable authority within. Why would we abandon them, drop our defenses, and render ourselves vulnerable when these protective mechanisms have brought us this far?

In addition, traditional cultures have all recognized the power of invisible energies, sometimes calling them spells, states of possession, or malevolent forces that must be propitiated, fled, or suffered irredeemably by a captive soul. Indeed, when Jung talked about how a complex can usurp control of the ego he used the German word *Ergriffenheit*, "the state of being possessed." When we are in the grip of a powerful complex, we are a possessed city-state, experience its occupation through our bodies, and serve its program by repetitive enactment of its instructions. Given that the complex is also a splinter script, no wonder the pattern is reinforced since that historically generated program is unchallenged in its power. Each time we serve the complex, its power is ratified and reinforced.

One of the ways in which this haunting occurs in each of us is the reactive patterns from mother and father. After all, are they not our primal models, our role enactors? And not just in imitative ways. We are just as much at the mercy of what they do not do, what is forbidden, or what is frightening to them. In the face of the unlived life of any parent or role model, we too are driven to repetition, are governed by a drive to escape that limitation in overcompensation, or fall victim to our unconscious treatment plans that generate a life of addictions, distractions, or compulsive agendas to breathe free.

Similarly, many suffer the lingering effects of deprivation, which diminish one's sense of legitimacy and permission to stretch into one's own possibilities. Others feel contaminated by guilt for things done or things undone, and this noxious emotion shuts them down or forces them to overcompensation. Still others feel driven by shame to repeat its toxic corrosion or to treat this devouring affect in patterns of overcompensation. And others feel marked by betrayals, disappointments, or disillusionments past and fritter away today's possibilities in regret, paralysis, and recrimination. It is as if *one is defined by a past sense of oneself rather than as a person who can learn from the past, learn what works and what doesn't work.* It is an abrogation of our essential freedom to begin each day with new possibility, new choices, new outcomes. No one would dream of walking backward down the street, but many times we do, haunted by, defined by a dismal past, rather than the lambent possibilities of a new day.

We are as a culture also haunted by the ghosts of constructs past. For my parents and my parents' parents, such constructs as gender, economic class, racial, religious, ethnic, and economic categories were thought ontological in character—that is to say, given either by nature or by divinity. Given the normative powers of culture, children are labeled, categorized, and treated according to those localized constructs, until they become exempla of those formative forces. The deconstruction of those received categories has steadily progressed through the last century into our own, yet they retain staying power in many minds. Slowly, these stereotypes are challenged by gifted individuals, appellate judicial review of prejudices ensconced in local law, and our own insurgent imaginations. Slowly, the right of the individual to self-determination is increasingly possible, yet still these lingering categorical chains haunt all of us. While time is on the side of increasing liberation of the human spirit, none walking the planet this day will fully feel the freedom to be oneself, so subtle are these invisible threads that bind the spirit to its fearful past.

Perhaps the greatest haunting of all is found in our collusion with the vagaries, velleities, and vacillations of our past. We all learned, as we know, that we were relatively powerless in a world beyond our capacity. We all learned that our survival at worst and our acceptance at best depended on acclimation to whatever the environment dictates. In the news of the hour in which I write this sentence, members of a fundamentalist church, including the parents, have been arrested for beating one of their children to death and gravely injuring a second. What was their children's outrageous crime? As now young men, they were seeking to leave the reservation, step out into the world as free.

How terrifying to the terrified such a choice becomes. If our children depart our ranks, how solid can our own footing be? But such a formulation, obvious as it is, is a step too far for those living in fearful embrace of simplistic categories, and they seek to destroy their own fears by destroying their own children. How great that fear must be, how shallow their grip on their own souls, that they should thus violate the central task of every parent to protect their young.

In every culture, there are stories, laws, customs, and sanctions that seem venerated by time and common practice which a later age will find arbitrary, ideocentric, and sometimes grotesquely violating of the human spirit. Pious souls have and continue to condone slavery, human trafficking, and discriminations of all sorts, yet we claim we are an enlightened society? Such are the hauntings that infiltrate our world and decay our souls.

We only begin to confront these hauntings when someone gets in our face and confronts us with the evidence of our behaviors, attitudes, and consequences; or when we have haunting dreams, dreams that speak to us of our unlived lives or confront us with our constricted range of choices; or when we find ourselves gripped by strange moods, seemingly not triggered by external events. Sometimes we find that all that we do and have done still produces ennui, a lack of satisfaction, a dysthymia. In such moments, our tendency is to redouble our efforts, and the disaffection multiplies. Or we anesthetize our internal discord with drugs or distraction, or we look for tangible people to blame out there somewhere. Only when the distress reaches a certain proportion are we likely to look within, to reexamine the principles and perceptions that govern our lives, or to enter a serious self-examination. Yet it is in those moments that the opening to a larger life begins.

Perhaps the biggest haunting of our lives is the overlearned fact of relative powerlessness in a world of giants and mysterious, inexplicable, and inexorable powers. What is lost in this appraisal is, of course, the contrary fact that there is a magnitude of possibility in each of us, a core strength, an abiding resilience that brings us to the summons of life with an ever-increasing capacity to take it on. Earlier this day, in doing supervision with a therapist considering her cases, we observed how some people find the resilient capacity to survive abuse, the loss of cherished others, and wounds to their self-worth, while others are blown away by the same events. It appears that it is not what happens to us, but how we internalize what happens to us, how we message it. What breaks some souls seems to energize others with resolve and determination.

While learned helplessness is one of the functional definitions of depression, we all learned helplessness in our childhood experience. For some, this learning was truly traumatic and invasive, but even those most injured by life often demonstrate a renewed capacity for growth and development, an overwhelming resilience. Rather, these childhood experiences, containing considerable energy as they do, may fuel resolve to confront, push through, persist in the face of the obstacles life presents. Few things will outlast the truly resolved, persistent person. I know this for a fact, not only personally but also in the lives of decades of clients. We cannot give this strength to another, but we can mirror it in ourselves and remind others, stimulate and reinforce the inherent powers granted us by the life force. We learn by going though these fears, not by running from them and thereby ratifying their preemptive powers.

In the end, we are haunted by the examples of the past, the denied permission to live a free journey. We are haunted by the partial examples of those in our purview, taking their pusillanimity or oppression as predictive of our own. We are haunted by the social constructs that tell us what a woman is and what she can or cannot do, and what a man is and how he will be shamed by living beyond these calculated constrictions. We are haunted by bad theology, bad psychology, and bad social models into thinking we are defined by our history, by our race, or by cultural heritage. We are haunted by the unexamined lives of our ancestors and caregivers. We are haunted by the widespread impression that history is the future. We are haunted by the limited imagination of our complexes. And even more, we are haunted by the small lives we live in the face of our immense possibilities. Haunting is individual, generic, cultural, and extremely hard to challenge because it so often seems bound by generations of practice, ancestral fears, and archaic defenses of privilege.

The biggest haunting of all, the biggest shadow that occludes our sense of sovereignty in the outer world, is the specter of our unlived life. Something within each of us suffers, longs, despairs, persists, and even goes underground to reemerge as fantasy, as projections onto surrogate objects of desire, or as anesthetizing self-soothing. When the soul is not honored, when our possibility is denied by an outer oppressor, a social proscription, or worse, our own pusillanimity, our pathology intensifies. We are bombarded with pharmaceutical anodynes, cultural distractions, and rationalizations and evasions that facilitate these deflections from the summons to personhood. In the context of such hauntings, the greatest ghost for us is the apparition of what was possible but that we shunned. Such moments are not very pretty and may have to haunt us even more to get our actionable accountability. If we live in haunted houses, we are called to turn the lights on and clean house.

# Chapter 16

# Free Your Children from You

Perhaps the key measure of successful parenting, despite whatever mistakes we have made, is whether our children really understand that we love them as they are, not as we wish them to be. This rather simple test is much harder to meet than it first appears. To be able to pull back our expectations of them—that they make us proud of ourselves, that they ratify our religious, political, and cultural values—first requires that we are really addressing the task of our own individuation and not imposing our unfinished business on them. Jung's observation that the greatest burden the child must carry is the unlived lives of the parents is chilling, frankly, for it puts all the responsibility for growing up back on me. In order to be a good parent, apparently I have to be a more evolved person in the first place.

The Little League father who screams at his son to play better ruins his son's potential love for the game. No matter how much he grows or achieves in life, that child will remember those moments when he failed to please his father. I have seen many a man recall remarks, criticisms, expectations from decades ago, and carry those shaming moments into much that he does or fails to do today. Those shaming moments show up in aversion to legitimate risk, overcompensation through risky behaviors, or pain-numbing addictions. The stage door mother who pushes her daughter to ballet lessons, or the piano, or cheerleading, in a vain effort to redeem her own sagging sense of self has the same impact. Even the death of the parent does not erase this feeling or reporting to a presence that can grant or withhold praise and acceptance. Whatever the intent, whatever the rationalization, such parents load their children's journey, perilous as it already is, with guilt, shame, failure, unbidden criticism, and a obsessive-compulsive drive to compensate elsewhere.

Most parents, even to this day, wish their children to grow up in the same religion, even when that religious confession is seldom practiced in daily life. We all know that most people espouse a personal religion based on the fortuity of their geographic and tribal births and not from genuine religious encounter or authentic personal election. Apparent security is promised in numbers and group identification and is narcissistically promoted when dictating one's children follow a path similar to one's own. Putting it bluntly: I am a good parent, a successful parent, if my child follows my path, reaches similar choices and lifestyle as I, thereby ratifying the rightness of my *exemplum* to them. What is the basis of that thought, common to most parents, other than personal insecurity? And how can insecurity be a firm basis for a parent-child relationship—not to mention genuine religious or values discernment?

Virtually every client with whom I have worked over the last four decades has had to struggle mightily to find a personal path, a journey that is right for him or her. They all find their journeys impeded by parental limitations, pressures, and models. And just as they struggle to find the permission, the sources of insight, and the guidance to chart their own course, so it may be readily imagined that their children will want the same freedom. In short, how can we grasp our possibilities, live our own authentic lives, if we do not model and grant overt permission for our children to live the separate journeys sought by their destiny?

I wrote in *The Eden Project* of what I call the heroic summons—namely, to lift off the intimate other the unfinished business of my own life. This I call heroic because it asks me to assume a burden much larger than feels comfortable. It asks that we outgrow the dependent part that is covertly eager to have someone take care of us. So we seek, unconsciously, to convert our partners into the good parent, the one who takes the task of self-esteem, of personal accountability, the responsibility for meeting most of our own needs, off our shoulders. Similarly, a far more unconscious, far more insidious but equally heroic task remains for parents—namely, to lift off our children's shoulders the unfinished business of our own lives. The more we do so, the more we free them to be.

Those parents who phone their adult children several times a week are sending a message: you can't live your own life, because you can't do it without my advice and counsel and because you always have to live with your eyes looking backward worrying about me. All of this leaves the child/adult guilt ridden, insecure, angry, and constantly diverting energy from the necessary tasks of their own life. Such persons are sabotaging their children, sending them disempowering messages, and making them nervously read the parent's whims for instructions, admonitions, and expectations. And could we ever call that good parenting, as such needy parents so often profess?

I recall one daughter who explained how she dreaded calling her mother. "How are you, Mom?" "Well, all right, I guess." The tone of course said to her daughter: drop everything you're doing in your life, and take care of me, daughter! On the other hand, there was the middle-aged man who came out to his parents, fearing the greatest wound gay persons ever have to suffer—the rejection of who they are by their parents. After he made his announcement, his father said, "Oh, thank goodness, and here I thought you were going to tell us you had become a Republican!" They all dissolved in laughter, and he knew that his mother and father loved him and that they were all going to move forward together.

I truly believe that the history of the world would change if we could just imagine parents healthy enough, wise enough, mature enough, evolved enough to say to their growing children something like the following: "Who you are is terrific. You are here to become yourself as fully as you can. Always weigh the costs and consequences of your choices as they affect others, but you are here to live your journey, not someone else's and certainly not mine. I am living my journey so you won't have to worry about me. You have within you a powerful source—call it your instinct, your intuition, your gut wisdom—which will always tell you what is right for you. Serve that, respect that. Be generous to yourself and others, but always live what is right for you. Life is really rather simple: if you do what is right for you, it is right for you and others.

If you do what is wrong for you, it will be wrong for you and others. Know that we may not always agree on things, and that is fine, because we are different people, not clones. Always know that I will respect you and value you no matter your choices, and you will always find here people who love you and care for you."

I believe that this message, however worded, would change the world because we would not have so many damaged people making their own babies in order to pass on their pathology. We would not have so many people turned violent because of the rage of their own troubled souls. We would not have so many self-defeating, avoidant, drug-addled, and unlived lives if people were not so estranged from their own souls. We would not have so many mindless folks who drift to politicians and preachers who offer them simplistic solutions to life's problems, give them people to blame rather than holding themselves accountable, and who give them ideologies to embrace rather than the legitimate risk and reward that living their own journey provides.

If we are ever going to free our children, as we wished to be freed from the web our parents may have spun for us, we have to generate our own lives. And if we really do love our children, as we profess, then we have to free them of our expectations that they live like us. Why should they? Is not our doing that sufficient? Why would they have to replicate our lives unless it was not about what it seems to be about, parental concern, but rather about our insecurity and what we have lacked the courage to face in our own lives?

Where I am stuck, my children will be stuck or will be diverting a significant amount of energy to compensate to get unstuck. Where I am bound by fear, by lack of permission, they will be bound. Where I am looking to others to help me evade growing up, either they will replicate my immaturity or become unduly burdened by responsibilities. As parents, mentors, leaders of one kind or another, we are called to grow up, take care of business, gain our own authentic journeys, and thus lift this terrible distraction to the soul off those whom fate has brought into our care. That is how we are healed, our children healed, and their possibilities liberated.

# Chapter 17

# Bestow Love on the
# Unlovable Parts of You

One of Jung's most important concepts is the idea of the *shadow*. The shadow is not synonymous with evil, though great evil can surely come from our shadows. Rather, I would define the shadow as those parts of us, or of our groups and organizations, that, when brought to consciousness, are troubling to our concept of ourselves, contradictory to our professed values, or intimidating in what they might ask of our timid souls.

Learning about and confronting our shadow is a central moral problem. This means that we have to be able to recognize our narcissistic motives, our cowardly retreats, and our slippery deal making with our values and still not be overwhelmed by guilt for our "unlovable" parts. I have always been moved by the two-millennia-old observation of Philo of Alexandria that we should be kind because everyone we meet has a really big problem. Remembering that allows me to be kind to many on this earth with whom I would otherwise have conflict. But I confess that I have trouble applying it to myself, given my expectations for myself. I cannot deny what I know. I cannot exempt myself from the radical scrutiny that I can apply to others, and I cannot evade accountability for whatever spills into the world through me. Thus, I find it hard to lend myself that respect, that level of forgiveness that I can so often grant to others.

Terence reminds me "nothing human is alien to me." So in my personal inventory, I must include the cheat, the coward, the lascivious, the penurious, even the violent. I may claim that I have never murdered someone, but perhaps unconsciously I have murdered my own potential, murdered my best dreams or those of others, or in my distractions and rationalizations, colluded in the many murders that go on in this world every day. Yet to acknowledge such complicity, such collusion, is to feel overwhelmed by sludge, reduced to a static, passive, even pathetic lot. Still, is it not the beginning of wisdom to recognize that what is wrong in the world is also wrong in me and that what must be righted in the world begins with me, rather than preaching to my neighbor?

Jung observed that a shadowless person is a superficial person. I have met a few persons through the years who claimed to have no shadow. They lived well, meant well, brought no overt harm to others, but they failed to see the nuances of their behaviors, the unintended consequences of their choices, or the pallid lives they conducted. One of the surest ways to learn something about our shadow is to ask those who really know us, perhaps those who live with us, to let us know what it is in us that annoys them, hurts them, impedes them. Not many of us would willingly invite such a potential indictment, yet it is played out every day in our relationships, through our children, and in our unwitting contribution to the pathologies of our times.

Anyone who becomes conscious over the years must occasionally look back and shudder: *What was I thinking? Why did I do that? Why did I not do what I knew I wanted to do then?* And so on. The list of particulars is as long as we have lived and continues to grow. Possibly the largest of the shadow issues still lies ahead. I find that the biggest shadow issue, that which people most resist, most rationalize away, most avoid, is the magnitude of the unlived life. As we just heard, Jung observed that the greatest burden the child must live is the unlived life of the parent. I suspect equally that the greatest burden our souls must bear is the unlived life. There is something in us, all of us, that knows what is right for us, which path is ours and not someone else's, something that pushes us beyond our comfort zone into areas of growth, development, and presence in this world greater than we have lived up to this point. We all have—to use the ancients' term—a daimon, a guiding spirit, a link to the larger energies, that courses not only through us but also through the universe. The daimon, as the ancients understood it, was a tutelary spirit, an agency linking the microcosm with the macrocosm. All of us have had this experience, especially in childhood, but when that voice, that prompting, comes later, it feels threatening because it asks too much of us, or at least it asks that which wedges us out of our comfort zones. It is in those moments that we defer, repress, or distract the inner voice and choose the more comfortable path. How many people have told me that they wish to do something, write a book, for example, and how many ever do it? They fail to understand that they have to lay themselves down before their fears and sacrifice their persuasive comforts to do so. They have to put aside self-doubt, bring the discipline necessary to every day, show up in a larger way than feels comfortable. And when they don't do this, something inside of them knows it and sours, mourns, grieves. And the more this flight occurs from whatever wants to live through us, the larger the shadow grows, the more intimidating our life becomes. After all, if I cannot face myself, admit my fears, and still wrestle with what wants to come into the world through me, how will I ever take on the outer fears found so readily in this world?

In the ever-growing inventory of self-criticism, we find it more and more difficult to forgive ourselves and to move on in service to life. Of course, there are those who move blithely through life, unaware and uncaring of consequences to themselves and others. Some of them are sociopaths and live in an arid emotional desert. They stopped feeling a long time ago. But most are not. They simply try to stay one step ahead of their lives, ahead of consequences, and have ready rationalizations that even they know are spurious.

But far more commonly, people sink under the weight of guilt, shame, or betrayal. These pernicious emotions represent a necessary recognition of harm done yet continue to poison the soul with the enervating toxins that impede change. While all the twelve-step programs promote a self-inventory, a laundry list of harm brought to self and others, they follow with the recommendation that one should seek confession and make amends with those harmed, when doing so would not bring further harm. That all makes sense. But one has to add one's own name to that list of those harmed, to the list of those needing amends and reparation.

Just as any of us may have regrets for things done and for things not done, so do we also have to see in what way the legacy of those choices continues to affect others, or perhaps continues to metastasize within us. Such unconscious compensatory treatments of this discrepancy can show up in anesthetizing behaviors, lives of distractedness, or lives of compulsive compensation. The unfinished business of the past can show up through the dominating business of the present. It can show up in our avoidance of new initiatives, our self-sabotage, our flight from engagement with various zones of sensitivity. Clearly, the past does not go away and is not past. Again, the real question is, What does it make us do, and what does it keep us from doing?

How can one say then that one must learn to love these unlovable parts? One of the paradoxes of the life of Jesus was his admonition to love the enemy, to embrace those who persecute us. How impossible an idea can that really be? Frankly, it is so impossible that most of his adherents don't even bother to try anymore and have ready rationalizations to legitimize this moral sleight of hand. To love the enemy would then ask me to love myself as my enemy as well.

If we are living in accord with our inner reality while simultaneously suffering the depredations of this discordant, dis-eased world, we nonetheless have supportive energies, clarifying affects, and a sense of purpose. When we get off track, these same manifestations turn against us. While the world rushes to pharmacology to numb the inner discord, the question remaining is simply and obviously this: What does the soul want, as opposed to our protective but regressive complexes? This simple question is intimidating because such an agenda can very quickly lead to the larger rather than the smaller in our lives, necessarily reframing our sense of what our life journey is about.

Anyone with a modicum of conscious awareness of oneself may discard self-respect as the first casualty of naiveté and inflation. But then how does one live a productive, growing life after that? Having a casual, untested self-esteem is overrated. If you are busy doing the life you are meant to do, rather than just being busy at being busy, you will find old questions of self-esteem slip into the background.

The more thoughtful we are, the longer the list of things that ask forgiveness. Given that it is so hard to forgive ourselves when we are sensitive to those around us, I have always drawn some leavening from the concept of grace. Theologian Paul Tillich expressed it best when he defined grace as accepting the fact that we are accepted, despite the fact that we are unacceptable.[1] Yes, given the accountability of a thoughtful, conscientious adult, our list of shortcomings is long indeed. And yet, given that we too are only human, sensitive, vulnerable, bound to our wounding history, then why can we not also lend a measure of grace to ourselves as we might readily to others? Since when are we exempt from the human condition? Why are we an exception to Philo's recommendation of kindness, given that we too are persons in a rather big crowd with really big problems? Why are we judged more than the other? Is not our radical condemnation of ourselves a narcissistic variant of our "specialness"? Is it not a form of peculiar narcissism to fault ourselves even more than others? Is it not a perverse satisfaction to deny to ourselves the grace we can bestow on others? Is it not a failure of love to be unable to love even the unlovable parts of ourselves?

The capacity to love our unlovable parts is not an endorsement but a recognition that they are also part of who we are. These troubling zones of the soul are what give form and depth to the human gestalt, without which we would be but creatures of our environment, automatons of "goodness," conditioned by overwhelming forces of sanction, social pressure, and accommodation. These parts are what give us character rather than the thin-souled one-dimensional creatures we were sometimes raised to be. These unlovable parts are what make us most human and therefore most worthy of grace and of love. Only grace, which accepts, and love, which heals, can ever lead us to a larger spiritual life, lest we remain mired in recrimination and derogation of the richness of the soul. Furthermore, paradoxically, only in the act of loving these unlovable parts of ourselves, which our ego consciousness sees as other, can we ever love others. This acceptance of others starts at home, by accepting the other that resides within us as well. I am still working on this myself, but I am working on it.

# Chapter 18

# Honor the Difference between
# Job, Duty, and Calling

D o we have a duty to duty? Yes, of course. To our jobs, for example, or a duty to our partners? Yes, again. Do we have a duty to calling? Also, yes. But what is the difference, and how do we tell them apart?

Put simply, jobs are how we earn our daily bread. We need jobs to pay the bills, support ourselves and others, and contribute to our world. I have cut grass, worked in the stockroom of a grocery, on an assembly line for a magnificent income of $1.75 per hour, cleaned houses for about $4 per hour, taught English to foreigners, and been a professor in a university, a professional writer, speaker, teacher, and psychoanalyst. The job of working on an assembly line many moons ago helped me learn how machines work, how assembly lines work, and, more importantly, how most men and women have to spend their lives, among them my good father. The jobs of cleaning houses and teaching English to foreigners occurred when I was a foreigner in someone else's country, sometimes working under the table and grateful to get cash to finance my studies and analytic hours. From them I learned the skills of survival, of counting pennies, and of discipline.

Given that both of my parents worked almost all of their lives was not only a model but also a critical lesson in reciprocity. They worked not only for themselves, for their own home and food, but also for me, and I never doubted that they sacrificed much in their souls so that my brother and I would have food on the table and clothing on our backs.

I never doubted that when I grew up I would not only do the same but also pay whatever price to be accountable to others as well as myself. To this day, I have more than one job. The difference today is that each job fuels the spirit and feeds the soul—and therein lies the tale.

Duty is where we acknowledge the legitimate claim that others make upon us. Duty is how we keep our society going. I have enormous admiration for those who rise in the morning and, aching in body and spirit, go off to work, perhaps leading Thoreau's "lives of quiet desperation," but nonetheless support themselves and those in their care. I am grateful for the souls running the buses that go down my street, for the fire, police, and civil servants who stand ready to help any of us at any time. I am grateful to the people who clean up our garbage, plow the snow off our streets, and keep all the systems running. I think of them every day in gratitude as we pass each other on the way to work. And I think of the elderly and the infirm, no longer capable of work, and thank them for reflecting on their lives and adding to the sum of what community really is. All of them are doing their duty.

In *Creating a Life*, I wrote of John Fowles's marvelous novel *The French Lieutenant's Woman*, set in the middle of the high Victorian era, when modernism bumped up against, eroded, and undermined the certainties of earlier times. In it, the central character is a conscientious man who is both a believer in his religious heritage and betrothed to a young woman aptly named Ernestina ("little Ernestness"). He is also a member of a new and emerging profession, geology. As he is exposed to the new fossil research that clearly undermines the certainties of his tradition—with its fanciful yet long-revered literal interpretations of scripture—and posits a world far earlier, beyond, and quite more complex than his tradition wishes to ratify, he is thrust into a conflict of duty. He has a duty to his religious values, and he has a duty to his professional calling as a scientist. What to do?

This dilemma is intensified by his encounter with a woman of suspect reputation with whom he falls in love. He is bound to his duty to Ernestina and bound to the binding legal contract that betrothal then meant. Breaking such a contract made him subject to legal sanction and worse, public calumniation and exile. What to do?

Jung observed that most of our neuroses, our deeply painful internal splits, arise because we experience the push-pull of legitimate duties. In the end, Charles, the geologist, has to make very painful choices; he ruins his career and reputation and loses both women. I leave it to the reader to read the full story and get why. Sooner or later most of us encounter tough choices and suffer greatly. Again, Jung commented on this kind of dilemma. To choose either A or B casually is to violate the legitimate claim of the other. His advice is to suffer the tension of opposites within ourselves as long as we can bear it and to wait upon the appearance of the "third." And what is the third?

In the choice between A and B, where each lays legitimate claim upon our duty, the third embodies the discernment of which choice summons us to a more developmental journey. Thus, for example, many fine folks feel honor bound to see to their parent's well-being, and well they should. However, many times this duty is an old complex that produces an inordinate amount of anxiety construed as guilt, as we saw earlier in this book. Sometimes the price of the parent-child nexus is so costly, the atmosphere so toxic, that the child has to walk away to save his or her life. Sometimes the child-*cum*-adult has to walk away to secure his or her own journey when the parent narcissistically demands and guilts the child into submission.

In relationship A or B, when one of the parties outlives the operative conditions of the relationship, what is he or she to decide? In one case, leaving is an example of immaturity, of flight, and he or she needs to remain to work something through that remains unresolved. In another case, he or she needs to leave, for remaining is succumbing to the claim of the complex, to duty as mere obligation, and remaining for this reason abrogates his or her own psychospiritual integrity. We cannot dictate either conclusion for another from the outside. Contrary to public perception, it is not the therapist's job to "save the marriage." It is the therapist's duty to help each party identify through honest suffering and difficult discernment what the third is for them. When both parties faithfully pursue this process, I have found that most can agree on the resolution: to continue in an evolved way or to dissolve with understanding and good faith on both sides. While we all have complexes around abandonment and disappointment, some of the best work therapists can do is help distressed parties reach an understanding that while there is a duty to duty, there is also a duty to the soul's truth, whatever it might be.

When we figure soul into the mix with job and duty, we then raise the question of vocation. Vocation derives from the Latin *vocatus*, meaning "calling" or "to be called." Ego consciousness does not do the calling; rather, the ego, the whole person, is called. Called by what? God, nature, the soul? Use the metaphor you prefer. *Called* means that that ego consciousness, fragile and frangible, nervous and driven, fixed or flowing as it is in any moment, lives at all hours in a larger context. Part of what it means to be an emergent adult is to realize both the tiny place our ego holds, like a fragile cork floating on a tenebrous sea, and the immense summons to which it is accountable. The ego is, after all, obliged to make choices every hour, whipsawed as it often is between competing force fields. All of our systems, our ethics, our jurisprudence, and our moral visions hold ego consciousness accountable for whatever spills into the world, even when it comes from our unconscious. I cannot say to the judge, "That came from my unconscious, and therefore I am not responsible." No civilized system permits us to get away with that slippery ploy. So we remain accountable to the world, to our daily life, to each other, and to our own soul. Sometimes these disparate claims upon us are in accord, and other times they occasion enormous suffering to us.

Vocation is our duty to our calling. In some cases, individuals are fortunate to bring together job and duty and calling in a unified form. I am one of those fortunate individuals, and while it was not always the case in my history, it has been for many years now. Every day I am grateful for that. My job of earning a living, my duty to contribute to the world in which I live, and my vocation to be a teacher in the sundry forums of classroom, book, and therapy are one, a seamless web, most of the time. I never forget that privilege afforded to me by having been born in a time when a poor child might through dint of education and persistence work to create a life much more satisfying than that experienced by his or her predecessors. Most of humanity has not had this opportunity.

Jung's concept of individuation is meant to be seen in this light—namely, as a duty to the soul. One is not thereby granted permission to narcissistic self-indulgence or spared brokenness of spirit by flight from the norms of one's time and space, but rather to the sacrifice that genuine vocation so typically requires. Some measure of suffering is demanded wherever vocation summons a person. For Jung, the idea of individuation is not about ego sovereignty but about sacrifice. But what is sacrificed? What is sacrificed is ego comfort, the easy path, the well-worn trailway. As a noted example, Dietrich Bonhoeffer had an easy life teaching at Union Theological in New York, but he also had a vocation. And he served it by returning to his homeland, then captained by a bunch of thugs and know-nothings, to speak against the horrors of the Third Reich. He ended his days as a victim of those moral slum-dogs, but he served his calling of faith. In one of his letters, he asked not that his God would rescue him from his captors but that he could have the courage and the insight to work his way through to what God asked of him in that terrible time and place. That he did, and that he bore witness to his soul's truth is why we honor him today, and so many others of large soul.

Most of us will not live such dramatic lives, yet every day we are called to decide what kind of human being we will be. We don't have to think very much, really. We can just let our daily legitimate duties carry us. We can let our acquired complexes unfold their historically generated programs for us, and generally, we will fit in, be missed when we pass, and contribute whatever we were duty bound to produce, though we will never have stood in the presence of the large.

Individuation is not about bold deeds on the large canvas of history, at least not for most of us. Individuation might actually be much more difficult than that. Individuation may be simply trying to show up as ourselves more days than not. All we are asked to do by history, the gods, nature, or by fate—whichever metaphor you prefer—is to show up as who we really are. Who we really are is not meant to fit in, be normal, imitate someone else's life. After all, that has already been done, so why repeat it? Individuation is the summons to grow up, to achieve personhood, to be a mensch.

Individuation means we contribute our idiosyncratic, eccentric, not-fitting-in-fully selves to this world. We deprive the mosaic of history whatever our tiny chip brings to the puzzle when we abrogate, flee, shun, or finesse our callings as souls. All of us know in some deep sense what our soul asks of us, what is most profoundly the right path for us, however perilous it might seem. Responding to what we know, trying to live it in our often inadequate, even broken, ways is all that life asks of us. Life asks of us jobs to earn our way, duty to serve the ties that connect us, and vocation to contribute the incredible richness that each person brings to the long trek upon which this species is embarked, and in the face of which we have so far yet to go.

# Chapter 19

# Construct a Mature Spirituality

S pirituality is one of the most slippery terms of our time. What does it mean? How does it differ from religion? Are they the same, or are they in conflict? And how can we identify spirituality, especially a mature spirituality? And who is to say which is which?

To address these questions, we first have to raise the question of authority. Who is authorized to make these decisions—ourselves or someone else for us? And what if that authority is inconsistent with our own reality or that which lies deep within us? Historically, the authority lay in the tribe, informed by its elders, its ancestors, its venerable stories. That other tribes had equally compelling authorities, sacred traditions, and the like is only a problem if one asserts the superior truth of one's own received authority and denies the received authority of the other. Or as Joseph Campbell wryly observed: myth is other people's religion.

Sadly, most tribalism, up to and including the tumultuous religious wars of our own age, again demonstrates the core insecurity of this human animal, who cannot get beyond his own internal security management and falls back on the primitive defense that "I am right, and you are wrong," or "My God is the true God, and your god is an imposter." That we have been at this sorry spectacle of complex-ridden, tribalistic religious wars for the whole of human history says something about our general difficulty in accepting ambiguity or the premise that the only way to respect the mystery is to allow it to remain the Mystery—without seeking to privatize it, codify it, and make it one's own. The hidden hubris behind such theologies is so overt that it is embarrassing to a thoughtful person, but one cannot overemphasize the power of human anxiety to commit the most appalling gymnastics of mind to justify anything.

What passes for popular religion in America, and many developed countries, is a rather pathetic encounter with the complexity of being human in an essentially unknowable universe. The largest religious groupings show up in two forms. One branch infantilizes its flock by making them feel guilty, reminding them how they failed to measure up to impossible standards of moral perfection. This stratagem is infantilizing because it activates the parental imagoes inside the head of most of us. Once evoked, this parental imago threatens both punishment and the withdrawal of approval, either of which proves devastating to the child. That such material is so easily evoked is an indication of how ineffective much parenting is—that the child does not feel a sense of personal worth and trust in the other. Such a dual betrayal of the legitimate needs of every person is repeated in pathologizing these "adults." They may walk around in big bodies, but inside is the terrified, invaded child. Shame on those who exploit this human vulnerability!

On the other hand, there are those slick, coifed types who tell people what they most want to hear: that you can have your wishes granted by right conduct, right thinking, right practice. While this hubristic, opportunistic quid pro quo was blasted to smithereens millennia ago by the wisdom of Ecclesiastes and Job, what sells better today than the wish fulfillment of modern materialism, hedonism, and narcissism? Why wouldn't any of us want to get right with the Big Guy upstairs, who can shower largesse upon our small lives? This "theology" is disguised boosterism, sales pitching, and motivationalism, and it ratifies greed, narcissism, and the desire for a stroll on easy street. What double trauma will these people experience when the real world happens again, as it always does, to refute the easy sales motivation of these slick promoters, for whom the only excess is the bulging coffers of their private fortunes? Shame on those who exploit this human vulnerability!

For any individual to construct a mature spirituality, it may be necessary to sort through the ruins of many great traditions, East and West, for they all have great wisdom embodied in their stories and exemplary figures. In the end, "the modern" is a person who understands that, for good or ill, the responsibility for spirituality has shifted from tribal religion to the shoulders of the individual. While this is an enormous freedom, indeed a privilege—a proffering of dignity to the human soul—it is also an intolerable burden for many. Such a person then has to ask what accords with his or her inner reality and reject what may speak to others but not to him or her. Never in recorded history has there been such a mythological crisis for so many; never in human history have so many been free to decide their path and what constitutes authority to them.

The human project is bathed in mystery: From whence do we come, whither to, and in between, what are we to do? These questions are universal and timeless. Each of us is called to address them for ourselves. If we do not, then we are either automatons serving the pressures exerted around us or have deferred our authority to someone else. Any encounter with genuine mystery, whether in the cosmos, in the intricacy of the atom, in each other, or even in ourselves, is an encounter with the radical other, so radically other that we will never know it for sure. If we did, it would not be the Mystery but a petty artifact of human construction.

We need to consider for a moment the phenomenology of the encounter with mystery. When we are in the presence of the genuine other, we are moved, shaken, stirred, attracted, or terrified, as the case may be. What arises from that phenomenological experience is the epiphenomenon—namely, the image that arises from the experience and generates our vehicle for relating to the transcendent other. The image and our understanding, however provisional, are not the Mystery; they are the by-products of the Mystery. Still, it is in the nature of human ego consciousness to fixate upon that image or that provisional formulation as a testimony to our need to demystify things, to understand them, perhaps even to control them. But in so doing, we reify, harden, concretize the image or the understanding, and in time are wed to the epiphenomenon, not the Mystery. So we codify and institutionalize our experiences, and the more we operate within these tertiary elaborations, however sincere our intent, the more removed we are from the Mystery itself. One of its more sinister consequences is thus the conviction of righteousness one possesses in denouncing the experience of others. As writer Anne Lamott sagely observes, we can conclude we have made our god in our own image when it turns out that our god hates the same people we do.[1]

These questions naturally require the sincere person to take Freud's blunt critique of religion very seriously. He opined that most, if not all, religion is the projection of parental complexes and infantile relational patterns onto the blank screen of the universe. Equally, it is the effort to establish security in this perilous transit by positing an afterlife and a longed-for paradisal state. Freud may not be wrong, per se, if one examines the psychological roots of one's own religious formulations.

But I think him not wholly right either. There is truly a place in the life of the human animal for wonder, curiosity, and openness to the fathomless otherness of the universe. This spirituality is found in the artist when she suspends her ego controls and paints the images that rise from unknown zones. It is found in the scientist reflecting on the intricacy of the molecule or the whirling planets and constructing an even better model than the one that served before. It is found in the parent holding the child in his arms for the first time, watching this fragile thing breathe on its own and knowing the whole human story is packed within and wishing to unfold. It is found every time we are drawn to encounter the mystery of each other and the infinity of possibilities that lie within us. We do not need another life, another universe, for this one is more than we can ever explore in our short dance here.

I submit to the reader that a mature spirituality will be found in the five following points.

First, it is the nature of the modern and the postmodern world that, like it nor not, one now has a responsibility that was once tribal. The flight from this accountability is a flight from oneself and deference to the received authority of others. So the first test of our trial-and-error process is found in the principle of resonance. Resonance means "to re-sound." When we try on someone else's coat, it may or may not fit, may or not accord with who we are, and so we readily change coats but do not accept anyone else's coat without it feeling right to us. If something is right for us, it resonates. If it is not right, it does not resonate. We can will it to do so, and even convince ourselves, but it won't pass the test of time. Often what seemed to resonate in the past ceases to do so presently, which is why so many have turned to the superficial and seductive images of secular society. But if something truly resonates within us, it is right for us, at least for now. Tomorrow will answer to tomorrow. Thus it is not with guilt or fear that we let go of yesterday's conviction, but with honesty about whether or not resonance occurs. We do not choose that; the soul makes that decision for us.

Second, a true spirituality opens up to the numinous, a word that speaks to something approaching us, soliciting our engagement, not willed by the ego. This means that even traumatic experience can be and often is numinous, because it hits us with the radical mystery of the other and obliges us to reframe our sense of self and world.

Third, mature spirituality opens us to mystery, which means certainty is a luxury of the naive, the frightened, the obtuse. This means that I must live with more uncertainty than is comfortable, and however unsettled I may feel, to realize that I have no honest choice but to go on and engage life and death on their terms, not mine.

Fourth, a mature spirituality asks me to grow up. We all know that a frightened child, an adaptive history, makes most of our decisions. We all know with what timidity we approach our lives, with what "checking in" we question our decisions, and what infantilizing wishes for magic drive our imaginations. Growing up, at the least, means that we accept full responsibility for our lives. We are, all of us, still responsible for meeting our needs, not some magical other, someone who will fix it for us, lift the burden off us, explain what it all means, instruct us in what we are supposed to do, and if we are really lucky, take care of us so that we don't have to grow up after all.

Fifth, our beliefs and practices are to be measured not by whatever solipsistic or seductive certainties they offer us, but whether they open us to mystery, deepen our engagement with the unfolding of our journey, and require us to grow up, live without certainty, yet conduct daily life with values that we do our best to practice.

In 1937, Jung gave the Terry Lectures at Yale University, and he concluded his three presentations by saying, "No one can know what the ultimate things are. We must take them as we experience them. And if such experience helps make life healthier, more beautiful, more complete, and more satisfactory to yourself and to those you love, you may safely say, 'This was the grace of God.'"[2]

To that I might add that such experiences of the other are sometimes reassuring, sometimes terrifying, but wherever they oblige us to reframe our stories, refashion our understandings, and crack us open to the new, we are in the presence of mystery. While this is seldom easy or pleasant, it is the opposite of infantilizing, the opposite of ratifying our narcissistic agendas. It is in such encounters with the universe in its unfolding mystery that we either grow spiritually or diminish. We either embrace the mystery of this journey, or we run from it. And something within us always knows the difference.

# Chapter 20

# Seize Permission to Be
# Who You Really Are

Recently I entered a supervisory session with a quite mature, gifted, experienced therapist, who is eminently thoughtful and qualified to do this work. She presented the case of a woman who is in a terribly one-sided marriage with a narcissist spouse, one for whom there is only criticism and derision of his wife's therapist. Of course, we know his terrible secret: he is terrified of self-examination because, as a narcissist, he already suspects there is no real core identity within. Such persons survive by control, domination, manipulation, passive-aggressive strategies, and the like, and cannot bear the strong light of consciousness upon themselves. Both of us agreed that the woman knows full well what she is married to, but inexplicably she is unable to do very much about it. She offers the lame rationalizations, which come so readily at hand to justify her paralysis: her friends were married and having babies while she was not, her vows promised "for better or worse," and so on. The fact that her own father fit a similar profile renders her even more powerless to acknowledge and leave, for it would mean that she might go through her history of abandonment again, even though it would rise out of her strength. We talked about this stalemate and reviewed how many other cases we had of such resistance to what the clients knew to be true. Even though this woman's psyche has already spoken to her, already made the judgment that the marriage is not healthy for her, and registered its disapproval through her psychopathology, she prefers to retreat from the abyss of choice.

So many other clients we both have treated have similarly been stuck. One reason for this internal division, this enormous resistance to undertake the obvious, lies in the power of the complex—that is to say, the recalcitrant powers of history to bring us back to the same old, over and over again. Each visit reinforces the theme: this is your history; you are your history; your history is your road map for the future; your fate-bound history begets your destiny. Were it not for psychopathology—that is, the recrudescence of a commentary from within—we would have to agree with this somber determinism. But psychopathology, again "the expression of the suffering of the soul," is a powerful contradiction to our adaptations to the world.

The implicit message for this woman, growing up with the parent granted her by fate, was, "You are powerless here. Your well-being will derive primarily from orbiting this large parental planet and accommodating to it. Do not expect to be met halfway by the other; you don't get that opportunity." This message was reinforced by the presence of an acquiescent mother, who also modeled adaptation over authenticity. After all, if the other "big person" cannot model a balanced relationship, what hope could there be for the child? Is it any wonder then, with this intrapsychic imago, this paradigm of self and other ingrained so deeply, repeated day after day through her formative years, that this woman would seek the familiar, a narcissistic partner, and fuse with him? And so she did, and so one does, because of two factors: the power of this unconscious conditioning and the lack of permission to live one's own journey.

This theme of powerlessness shows up time and time again as the inordinate influence of early models of self and world, self and other, and it shapes our inner paradigms. Even though the great religions endorse the notion of the soul, the preciousness of the human being, and even though the government of enlightened nations ratify the pursuit of life, liberty, and satisfaction, this issue of permission is critical. Many of us, most of us, were raised to be nice, to fit in, not to promote ourselves, and this somehow got translated into self-abnegation, self-criticism, and self-avoidance. It is not narcissistic to become—it is a duty. But who has ever heard that in his or her childhood? Very few, if any.

Permission is not something one receives from others, unless one had very thoughtful, very liberated parents who could affirm such a life journey for their child and model it themselves. Permission is denied by so many social constructs. Gender constrictions have been protested by women over the last few decades, and rightly so, but are equally constrictive to the emotional expressivity available to men as well. Men are at least a half century behind women in the arousal of consciousness regarding these permission-denying definitions. As I have said to more than one man, "You carry within a lake of tears and a mountain of anger and have been cut off from both, and you wonder now why you feel so bad and your relationship is so troubled."

Add to the constrictive powers of genderism such other procrustean pathologies as racial and ethnic constrictions, sexual and relational scaffolding, and socioeconomic structures, and we wonder why we are not comfortable inside our own skin and in our feeling life! Still, as we learned early, to push back is to risk either punitive responses or the loss of approval and support—both devastating to the fragile equilibrium of the child. So we learn to adapt, push the unlived life further below, and try to fit in. Outnumbered, the child gives in and thereafter deepens self-estrangement.

In the superficial world of most psychological practice in the Western world, we are defined as behaviors, which we are; thought constructs, which we surely have; and biological processes, which are self-evident. But such a definition of the human being leaves out the most important thing of all: we are a meaning-seeking, meaning-creating animal, an animal that profoundly suffers the disconnect from meaning. More symptoms arise from, more addictions bespeak, and more sociopathies testify to this disconnect than any other etiology. Over the last few centuries, and especially through the twentieth century into ours, mythic linkage to the mysteries have eroded and been replaced by secular surrogates and sundry distractions.

With greater freedom for more persons than anytime in the history of this planet, we have more souls adrift and more pathologies present as a result. As Jung put it in a letter once, we have fallen off the roof of the medieval cathedral into the abyss of the self. And he further noted that modern depth psychology, the discipline that seeks to engage the whole person, to dialogue with the inner world, "had to be invented" because of the mythic dissolution that threw so many unprepared millions back on their own resources.[1] Many seek the reinstitution of old values, old practices, which fail to hold up to modernism's relentless surge. Others relinquish the invitation to personal accountability and drown in the cacophonies of twenty-four-hour distractions.

In the face of this loss of tribal links to the mysteries, the question of permission persists with ever-increasing urgency. If we are to grow up, we have to take on the invitation to self-determination, dialogue with the inner voice, answer the summons to an authentic journey—all quite contrary to the instruction to fit in. Growing up means, among other things, that I am accountable for my life, my choices, my consequences. It is not enough to say, "I meant well." These choices came from me, from the values I professed, from the politicians I elected, the dubious choices I affirmed in the marketplace of ideas. There is no one who is going to show up and explain it all to me. I have to figure it out for myself and through trial and error and occasional suffering find a path, friends, values, lifestyle that are confirmed from within. No one knows what is going on, really. When we were children, we presumed the folks in the big bodies knew what was going on. Guess again. When we entered first adulthood, we presumed that the people in exterior authority knew what was going on and that they, whether priest or politician, had our best interests at heart. Guess again. Growing up requires that we accept that no one out there knows what is going on, that they are as much at the mercy of their complexes and unconscious mechanisms as the least of us, and so now we must figure it out for ourselves.

How many of us are still waiting for permission to be who we are, to live the journey meant for us in our mysterious incarnations in this world, to bring our small but critical chip to the large mosaic of history, our paragraph to add to the human story? Just when and where will that permission arrive? What is it we are waiting for? A new priest, another well-coifed guru, a compelling parent figure, maybe Elvis? And how long can we continue to fool ourselves, to think we are adults when we are still frightened children huddled within the towers of history, still waiting for instructions from the parent or parent surrogate?

What we need to know is already known within. Sometimes life circumstances require that we risk trusting that inner authority. Sometimes a therapist, in the transference that often happens in therapeutic relationship, embodies the permission-granting authority figure, the simulacrum of an empowering parent, but even that does not always work. Sooner or later, a person has to understand and revisit the basics: we are not here for long; we are accountable for the life we have lived or not lived; we are summoned to choice, courage, and perseverance in living this life. From that recognition, the necessity of permission becomes more than obvious; it becomes the vital oxygen we must breathe, or we choke to death on the fumes of the unlived life.

Once the question is asked, "Is this your life or someone else's, and are you responsible for it?" everyone mutters yes. And so, what is the problem then? Whose permission is needed to know what we already know? As Chögyam Trungpa puts it to us: "Self-deception often arises because you are afraid of your own intelligence and afraid you won't be able to deal properly with your life. You are unable to acknowledge your innate wisdom. Instead, you see wisdom as a monumental thing outside yourself. That attitude has to be overcome."[2] While we have hitherto noted that much comes between us and what we know, still our bones know, our blood knows, our dreams know, and sometimes we have to reach a point where we can no longer not know what we already know. And then the possible life opens before us, waiting only for our courage and resolution, waiting only for us to suit up and show up at last.

# Chapter 21

# Live the Examined Life:
# Live the Questions, Not the Answers

We all know that Socrates urged us to live "the examined life" and added that the alternative was not worth living. What is the examined life, and what is wrong with the unexamined life? What's wrong with hanging out, watching the telly, talking to friends online, getting stoned, and maybe getting laid from time to time? After all, we're all headed to the same place. Isn't the idea to pass the time as pleasantly as possible, especially since the world is always going to hell anyway, and there is nothing we can do about it?

As pleasure-seeking, pain-avoiding animals, we are also animals with the capacity for self-reflection, including being divided against ourselves and neurotic, as most of us are. But we can bring issues to consciousness and alter their course. The truth is, the unexamined life means that one is living not only unconsciously but also probably living someone else's life as well. Why? Because we are making choices every second, and if the choices are not the products of some differentiated consciousness, they will be driven by the complexes, by the archaic agendas of the past, remaining subject to the pressures of the moment. Either way, such a life is derivative, not generative, secondary, and not really ours.

We are the animal that suffers disconnection from meaning. We drift into avoidant patterns, we fall sway to the loudest voice in the crowd around us, or we slavishly serve the inner tapes that we inherit from family of origin, religious and cultural inculcation, and the persuasive powers of popular culture. In short, it is a derivative life, driven by invisible winds and subject to missed appointments with the soul, lost opportunities to explore the mystery we are in during this short time we have.

As children we all asked the elemental questions: Who am I, who are you, why are we here, what are we to do, and whither do we go? These questions are mostly forgotten, pushed into the suburbs of the busy metropolis of modern life. But they rumble on in the unconscious of us all. We look for them unconsciously in each other, in novels, in television shows, movies, and so on, or we anesthetize their loss in the thousand forms of busyness and distraction our culture provides.

This human animal is a creature of desire, and what it most desires is meaning, and what it most suffers is the loss of meaning. The autonomous judgment going on within each of us is a function of our psychospiritual reality. We can and often must mobilize ego energy and intentionality to address needful tasks, and the maintenance of society often requires us to do so. But mobilization that does not attend the needs of the soul inevitably leads to burnout, ennui, depression, and finally a deadening life. Such a life is sadly more the norm than we wish to acknowledge. Such a life is generally filling time until the guy with the scythe shows up at the door, as he invariably does.

When young, we believed the big folks knew what was going on, that there was a collection of knowledge that we could access to help us understand life, that explained what we were about, how we were to live, and how life could make sense to us. Little did we imagine in those hours of yearning that we grew more through the questions than any answers we might have received. Oh, the world had answers enough—there was no shortage of answers—but none of them fit anymore. After a while, one begins to suspect what is so obvious now: there are only answers to small questions. There are only answers that make sense to you at this moment in your life, and they will fail you later in your journey. What is seemingly true today will be outgrown tomorrow, when life or our own soul brings us a larger frame through which to view them.

One of the problems with complexes is that they have no imagination; they can only repeat the image latent in their formation and the epiphenomenal message that rose to account for that moment. But those moments are surpassed by other moments, other experiences, and other narratives that reposition our sense of self, our sense of world, and our relationship with each other. The plans, models, and expectations of yesterday are the prisons of today. And as Shakespeare noted, no prisons are more confining than those we know not we inhabit. Thus, good souls continue to assiduously apply old understandings to the new terrain of their lives with increasingly diminishing results. And the symptoms intensify. What the new terrain requires, the new stage of the journey demands, is as yet unknown, and thus sometimes we suffer the terrible interim between.

A substantial gift of the therapeutic arrangement is to construct a holding place whereby the deconstruction of the old may take place, exigencies of the moment be attended, and watchful attendance upon the emergent be supported. When approached in good faith, this process normally works because there is always a new plan that emerges from the depths of the soul, when we grow humble enough to wait upon it. Most of the people we admire most throughout history had difficult lives, but they share a common trait—namely, that they hung on until the new purpose of their lives emerged for them, and they found the courage to live those new challenges. That is why we admire them and also why we are called to do the same in our lives. What matters is that you live this life by the best lights you have, by what really matters to you, whether or not anyone around you understands or supports that.

What was most troubling to me as a child and as a young adult—namely, the presence of ambiguity and uncertainty—is today almost comfortable. This is because I have learned whatever makes sense today will be insufficient tomorrow when I have larger questions, larger contexts, and more consciousness to bring to the table. I also know, wherever there is "certainty," there either is naiveté, unconsciousness, or defense against doubt. Wherever there is a hysterical certainty, and there is much in our land, it is because doubt has already planted its black flag inside the soul and the ego is running away like a child.

In childhood, simple questions led to simple answers. Because the large questions led to ever-larger uncertainty, many of us shut down, stopped asking, and thereby stopped growing. But the same questions are still being asked in the unconscious: *Who am I? Who are you? What is all this about? Whither are we bound, and how am I to live my life?* When they percolate to the surface, they bring each of us a summons. The only question is, Will we keep the appointment? Many, perhaps the great majority, never keep the appointment, never show up, and thus lead lives of quiet desperation, suffer anesthetized souls, and have to continuously palliate distracted consciousness. Others show up because they have to. Keeping that appointment is where our lives find their purpose—not in answers but in living large questions that are worthy of the soul's magnitude.

And that is why the examined life matters.

# Afterword

It is my sincere belief that if the reader not only reads but also rereads one of these twenty-one suggestions on a daily basis, genuine growth will occur. At the very least, these ideas, obvious in themselves, are nonetheless calling us to accountability, to enlarged consciousness, when so much of daily life plows onward the same, driven by external pressures and the internalized scripts we all have.

These challenges are pragmatic and demanding and are shared in good faith, with a warm heart, and with sincere good wishes to the reader. Consider them; meet them anew in different contexts and stages of your life. Over time they may transform from ideas into changed internal structures that help you make different choices in the thousand forking paths you traverse each day.

As I reflect on these steps, I find them helpful in my approach to my life. I have shared them to some good effect with clients and audiences, and I share them now with other travelers on this journey we call our lives. There are many perils on this journey, and it ends in the great democracy of the grave—and yes, each of us has to make the journey on our own and by our own lights. But there are many—sometimes invisible—fine companions on that road, a worthy collection of thoughtful souls such as yourself, so you are not alone. Alone and together, our lives matter and make a difference.

# Notes

## CHAPTER 1   THE CHOICE IS YOURS

1. The night I write this sentence, a fundamentalist group has executed a professional archaeologist for his preservation efforts in the Middle East. What is his crime? He simply affirmed a cultural history outside the range of the immature, stunted imagination of fundamentalism, for which "the other" is always a threat.

## CHAPTER 2   IT'S TIME TO GROW UP

1. Marcus Aurelius, *Meditations* (Mineola, NY: Dover Publications, 1997), 77.

## CHAPTER 4   RECOVER PERSONAL AUTHORITY

1. Chögyam Trungpa, *Shambhala: The Sacred Path of the Warrior* (Boulder, CO: Shambhala Publications, 1984), 7.

## CHAPTER 8   COME BACK TO YOUR TASK

1. Carl Jung, "Psychotherapists or the Clergy," in *Collected Works XI* (Princeton, NJ: Princeton University Press, 1958), 330.
2. Jung, 336.

## CHAPTER 9   CHOOSE THE PATH OF ENLARGEMENT

1. Remember that genius comes from *genie*, the inherent spiritual presence in each of us. We all have such a presence, though we may have lost contact with it many years ago.

## CHAPTER 12    WHAT IS THE BIGGER PICTURE FOR YOU?

1. LearnVest, "The Salary That Will Make You Happy (Hint: It's Less Than $75,000)," *Forbes*, April 24, 2012, forbes.com/sites /learnvest/2012/04/24/the-salary-that-will-make-you-happy -hint-its-less-than-75000/#3a2e7a873247.

## CHAPTER 14    HONOR, FINALLY, WHAT YOU LEFT BEHIND, AND SEIZE PERMISSION TO BE WHO YOU ARE

1. *Wikipedia*, "Terence," last edited May 18, 2017, en.wikipedia.org/wiki/Terence.

## CHAPTER 17    BESTOW LOVE ON THE UNLOVABLE PARTS OF YOU

1. Paul Tillich, *The Courage to Be* (New Haven, CT: Yale University Press, 2000).

## CHAPTER 19    CONSTRUCT A MATURE SPIRITUALITY

1. Anne Lamott, *Traveling Mercies: Some Thoughts on Faith* (New York: Anchor Books, 2000), 22.
2. Carl Jung, "Psychology and Religion," in *Collected Works II* (Princeton, NJ: Princeton University Press, 1958), 105.

## CHAPTER 20    SEIZE PERMISSION TO BE WHO YOU REALLY ARE

1. Carl Jung, *Symbols of Transformation, Collected Works V* (Princeton, NJ: Princeton University Press, 1956), 25.
2. Trungpa, *Shambhala*, 54.

# Bibliography

Aurelius, Marcus. *Meditations*. Mineola, NY: Dover Publications, 1997.

Dostoyevsky, Fyodor. *Notes from Underground*. New York: Vintage Classics, 1994.

Fowles, John. *The French Lieutenant's Woman*. New York: Signet, 1970.

Hollis, James. *The Middle Passage: From Misery to Meaning at Midlife*. Toronto: Inner City Books, 1993.

———. *Tracking the Gods: The Place of Myth in Modern Life*. Toronto: Inner City Books, 1994.

———. *Creating a Life: Finding Your Individual Path*. Toronto: Inner City Books, 2001.

———. *Finding Meaning in the Second Half of Life: How to Finally, Really Grow Up*. New York: Gotham Books, 2005.

———. *Why Good People Do Bad Things: Understanding Our Darker Selves*. New York: Gotham Books, 2007.

———. *What Matters Most: Living a More Considered Life*. New York: Gotham Books, 2009.

———. *Hauntings: Dispelling the Ghosts Who Run Our Lives*. Asheville, NC: Chiron Books, 2014.

Hopkins, Gerard Manley. *Poems and Prose*. London: Penguin Books, 1985.

Jung, Carl. *Collected Works. Twenty Volumes*. Princeton, NJ: Princeton University Press, 1953–79.

———. *Symbols of Transformation, Collected Works V*. Princeton, NJ: Princeton University Press, 1956.

Lamott, Anne. *Traveling Mercies: Some Thoughts on Faith*. New York: Anchor Books, 2000.

Neumann, Erich. *Depth Psychology and the New Ethic*. Boulder, CO: Shambhala Press, 1990.

Rilke, Rainer Maria. *Poems of Rilke.* Translated by Stephen Mitchell. New York: Vintage, 1989.

Tillich, Paul. *Systematic Theology.* Chicago: University of Chicago Press, 1967.

———. *The Courage to Be.* New Haven, CT: Yale University Press, 2000.

Trungpa, Chögyam. *Shambhala: The Sacred Path of the Warrior.* Boulder, CO: Shambhala Publications, 1984.

Yeats, W. B. *The Tower.* New York: MacMillan Publishers, 1928.

# About the Author

J ames Hollis, PhD, is a Jungian analyst in practice in Washington, DC, where he is also executive director of the Jung Society of Washington. He lives with his wife, Jill, a retired therapist, and they have three living children and eight grandchildren.

# About Sounds True

Sounds True is a multimedia publisher whose mission is to inspire and support personal transformation and spiritual awakening. Founded in 1985 and located in Boulder, Colorado, we work with many of the leading spiritual teachers, thinkers, healers, and visionary artists of our time. We strive with every title to preserve the essential "living wisdom" of the author or artist. It is our goal to create products that not only provide information to a reader or listener, but that also embody the quality of a wisdom transmission.

For those seeking genuine transformation, Sounds True is your trusted partner. At SoundsTrue.com you will find a wealth of free resources to support your journey, including exclusive weekly audio interviews, free downloads, interactive learning tools, and other special savings on all our titles.

To learn more, please visit SoundsTrue.com/freegifts or call us toll-free at 800.333.9185.